The Scottish Footballers of Everton

1880-1915

Tony Onslow

First Published 2011 by Countyvise Ltd
14 Appin Road, Birkenhead, CH41 9HH

Copyright © 2012 Tony Onslow

The right of Tony Onslow to be identified as the author of this work has been asserted by him in accordance with the Copyright, Design and Patents Act 1988.

British Library Cataloguing in Publication Data.
A catalogue record for this book is available from the British Library.

ISBN 978 1 906823 64 1

Acknowledgements,

Donald Lindsay, Duncan Carmichael, Stuart (the Jag) Deans, Stewart Franklin and John Stewart

Maggie May, The Mitchell Library, Glasgow

Billy Smith, whose website, The Blue Correspondent, saved me a lot of time and shoe leather

Marie McQuade, whose help was invaluable

Dedication

Cathie Ferguson, a Loyal Scot from North Ayrshire

Introduction

This book tells the story of the lives and times of the many Scotsmen who wore the colours of Everton Football Club prior to the First World War. Most of them came from the traditionally industrial background that once existed in Scotland and provided the population with most of their employment. Many of them were forged in the Shipyards and Heavy Engineering works that once made up the central belt of Scotland while others laboured beneath the ground in the coalfields of Ayrshire, Lothian and Fife. Several of these football players also came from fishing ports and industrial Cities of the Eastern Seaboard of Scotland while one or two others hailed from the lowland border region of the land once known as Caledonian.

The male inhabitants of this North British nation, to fill in their leisure time, eventually began to embrace the new ball game that was played under the rules of the Football Association in London and the strange new word of soccer soon became part of Scottish vocabulary. This new pastime first took root among the middle classes of the Strathclyde region before spreading south into the Ayrshire coalfield and then eastwards towards the nation's capital and beyond. The game had first reached the Scottish nation via the public school system of England and soon football clubs sprang up all over central Scotland thus necessitating the need for a governing body similar to that already in existence in England. The Scottish Football Association formed in 1872 in Glasgow followed the pattern of the governing body which was already active in London. However, the new organization, unlike their English counterparts, was slow to embrace the ethos of professional football and for many years banned their members from being rewarded for playing the game they now referred to as "Fitba". The leading players then headed towards England and from as early as 1878 Scotsmen were reported to be working on the Plains of Albion where they supplemented their income by being rewarded for playing football in their adopted community.

The Scots were first reported to be playing football in the small mill towns of east Lancashire from where they gradually found their way to the clubs situated in the larger cities of England. One such club was Everton.

The Everton Scottish

Liverpool will always be famous for its Irish connections while the people of North Wales, along with those of Lancashire, have also played a large part in making the city what it is today. The Scots, however, have also made a contribution. In1890 the Liverpool & District St Andrew Society was formed and social gatherings were held at the Presbyterian chapels in Wavertree and Fairfield. The 1891 census revealed that there were 15,276 people living in Liverpool who had been born in Scotland and they made up nearly 3% of the population. Both Ireland and Wales have, over the years, furnished Everton Football Club with some excellent players but it is their Gaelic cousins from North of the Border who have provided the biggest percentage. The first of these invaders, a man from Glasgow, arrived in Liverpool sometime around 1880.

John McGill has, over the years, become a bit of an enigma because it had previously been thought that his birthplace was somewhere in Ayrshire. He was however, born on the banks of the River Clyde. McGill first saw the light of day, 25 2 1859, at 559 Gallowgate in the east end of Glasgow where he grew up under the watchful eye of his mother, Mary. He must have then served an apprenticeship in the engineering trade because, in 1881, he was living at 18, York Terrace in Everton where he declared his occupation to be that of an Engine Fitter. His sister Hannah is listed as head of the household and married to John Monteith a Glasgow born sea-going engineer sailing out of Liverpool aboard the *S S Palm*. It is around this time that Jack McGill is first reported to be playing football for Everton on Stanley Park.

The local newspapers of the period make reference to McGill as having joined Everton from Glasgow Rangers, but his name is not recorded as ever playing in the Scottish clubs senior eleven. Association Football was, at this time, thriving in Scotland and it is likely that McGill had played the game with one of the many

Glasgow clubs that where in existence long before he arrived in Liverpool. What is certain, however, is that he was engaged as a player/coach by Everton at the commencement of 1880/81 football season and was to figure prominently in the clubs formative years at Stanley Park. On the 17th October 1882 McGill was in the Everton side when they played an away Lancashire Cup against Blackburn Rovers on their former home ground at Leamington Road. Everton lost the game 8-1 but the efforts of Jack had not gone unnoticed. Sam Ormerod, a prominent member of the Lancashire FA, approached the Scotsman and persuaded him to join his hometown club, Accrington. McGill played several games for the East Lancashire club before returning to assist Everton in the Liverpool knockout where they went down to Bootle by 3 goals to 1. McGill remained loyal to Everton during their uncertain time at Priory Road and was part of the side that beat Earlestown to win the Liverpool Cup in 1884. Though principally a forward, McGill occupied the right back position when Everton opened their new ground at Anfield and played well as they beat the visitors by 5 goals to 0. He eventually lost his first team place and ended his football career playing with the Everton veteran eleven.

Jack McGill was soon to find a second home in Everton on the notoriously steep Haverlock Street where he succumbed to the charms of a local 21 year old widow lady named Mary Ellen, nee Argyle, Powdrell. They were married, 5 1 1887, at the parish church of St Peters and set up home at 21 Rydal Street where they began to raise a family. Jack continued to work in engineering while maintaining close links with Everton Football Club where he turned out in the annual Married v Single players football match. The McGill family eventually made their home at Kempston Road in Wavertree where, on the 17th of January 1937, Jack died at the age of 67 and was buried at Smithdown Road cemetery. His wife and three daughters survived him.

Tom Veitch made a guest appearance for Everton on the 29th of August 1885 in their match against Great Lever. He had recently joined neighbours Bootle from his local club Dumbarton with whom he had twice previously toured Lancashire. Veitch partnered George Dobson at full back but could not prevent Everton from avoiding a 1-0 defeat. He made a second guest appearance on 28 4 1887, when he came in as a last minute replacement for the injured George Dobson against Preston North End at Anfield. He went on to play over 100 games for the Bootle club and eventually, became their captain before ending his playing career with Lancashire League side Heywood Central.

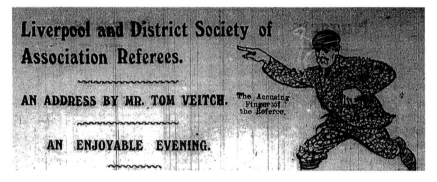

Tom Veitch later became one of the leading and most respected referees in the Liverpool area. He eventually settled, with his Irish born wife, at 110 Gloucester Road in Bootle and obtained employment as a shipwright on the Liverpool Docks. He became a lay preacher at his local Methodist chapel and was much sought after as a speaker during the years leading up to the First World War. In 1907 he is reported as addressing a temperate meeting that went under the title of a "Football Sunday" that was held in a hall close to the Everton ground. Tom Veitch spoke of the derby games that once existed between Bootle and Everton that, in his words, were much hotter than those of today. He said he was a "person who believed that Christianity and football could and should be dovetailed for he said that he still loved the grand old game". The old time Bootle defender reiterated his defence of football professionalism very tellingly and convincingly when he gave as his reason "because I know something of the sham amateurism of 20 years ago" He said "The Scot loved his country but was not averse to bettering himself" and also stated that "When I crossed the Tweed I took one fond look at the land of my birth and then turning right about face exclaimed, "The World is my Parish".

GLASGOW & SOUTH-WESTERN RAILWAY.

NEW-YEAR HOLIDAYS.

CHEAP EXCURSION TO

Liverpool, Manchester, Leeds, Bradford, Blackburn, and Bolton,

ON WEDNESDAY, 31st DECEMBER,

By SPECIAL EXPRESS TRAIN leaving KILMARNOCK at 9-0 p m.

RETURN FARES.

To	1st Class.	3rd Class.
Liverpool and Manchester,	20s.	10s.
Leeds and Bradford,	16s.	8s.
Blackburn,	16s.	8s.
Bolton,	18s.	9s.

Passengers return on 4th January (Sunday, Midnight) by Trains leaving Liverpool (Exchange Station) at 12 Midnight; Manchester (Victoria Station) at 12-15 a m.; Leeds at 12-45 a m.; Bradford at 1-0 a.m.; Blackburn at 1-10 a.m.; and Bolton at 12-35 a.m.

W. J. WAINWRIGHT, General Manager.

Glasgow, December, 1884.

Andrew Gibson was one of a small glut of players who came to Liverpool from the Kilmarnock area in the mid-1880s. He is first recorded playing football for Bootle, at centre half, in October 1885 and represented them in the Liverpool Senior Cup final against Everton on the 10th of April 1886. Gibson, who gave a wholehearted performance, could not prevent Everton from carrying off the trophy with a 1-0 victory. His spirited style of play, throughout the season, endeared him to the Bootle crowd and they were dismayed when, during the closed season, he transferred his loyalties to their main rivals Everton.

The Everton executive, who made Gibson a good offer, were anxious to find a replacement for Tom Fayer who had recently left the club and emigrated to New South Wales. The Scot was trusted in to the heart of the Everton defence when the club opened their new season with a visit from the powerful set of players assembled by Bolton Wanderers. He held his own as Everton went down by 3 goals to 1. Nonetheless, the transfer of Gibson appeared to rankle with a small section of the local football followers who saw his actions as being somewhat mercenary and this prompted a local journalist, in order to settle the matter, to put pen to paper…*Fayers position was taken - oh irony of fate - by the best hated man from the rival camp. Events move quickly in these fast times. It seems but yesterday when howls of execration greeted a certain stalwart Bootle player as he dashed with all his might at the defenders of the Everton goal. He was then a stiff un, and something very more uncomplimentary, but he is now well worth so much a week. If Andy's new friends have much to forget his old ones have learnt a lesson. It is not too much to say that amongst the followers of Bootle, Gibson was the most popular amongst the Bootle players. His election as vice captain is proof of this. No player either was ever profuse in his protestations of loyalty. Nobody will deny that a professional player has the right to offer his services to the highest bidder, but people have the odd knack of remembering that there are such old fashioned virtues - gratitude, friendships and loyalty and that such are usually considered as beyond expression in current coin (Liverpool Courier August 1886.).*

We notice that A. Dick and A. Gibson (both belonging to Kilmarnock) have been playing a final tie in Liverpool, and have been fortunate in securing gold medals. From an English paper sent us, we notice Dick has been very prominent, as he is repeatedly mentioned. Their team played with ten men nearly all the game, but won rather easily for all that. R. Stevenson was also a member of the same team up to the time of playing the final, but was hindered by business from taking part in the last game.

Andrew Gibson served Everton well during the short time he spent at the club. He played mostly at halfback and also did his best, when asked to do so, to play at centre forward. Gibson eventually got his Liverpool Senior Cup winners medal when Everton won the trophy in 1887. He also took part in the controversial FA Cup tie with Bolton Wanderers and was the only Scottish player, from the Everton team, not to be summonsed before the FA inquiry that followed the game. He appeared for Everton after their suspension and stayed with them until the end of the season. He then vanished off the radar and did not appear for Everton after they joined the Football League. Andrew Gibson, who spent the rest of his life in Liverpool, died, 6 11 1936 at 74 Melbourne Street, Everton. He was aged 76 and his wife survived him.

James Alexander Dick came to Merseyside in 1885, at the invitation of Stanley Football Club. Always known as Sandy, he previously played his football with Kilmarnock Athletic before accepting terms with the Merseyside club to join them on their home at Walton Stiles. He was a robust and fearless wee man whose uncompromising style of play was to soon earn him the nickname of "Dirty Dick". He captained the Stanley club before deciding to join the group of Scotsmen who were now gathering to play their football with rivals Everton at Anfield.

F O O T B A L L.

At the hour for starting the Lugar v. Athletic Ayrshire cup tie on Saturday last the Holm Quarry bore quite an unusual appearance. The attendance of spectators was not large, but very select, and in the palmy days of the Athletic they had seldom more followers round them than attended this match to see them stand or fall. Morton, Thomson, and Lochhead appeared as representatives of the past, M'Skimming and Wright (another pair from the nursery at Hurlford), Allan from Kilwinning, with Houston, Campbell, Dick, Pollock, and Whiteside made up the Athletic team. The Lugar have been likewise poaching from weaker brethren—Cumnock and Cronberry being

On 30th October 1886 Sandy was one of the ineligible members on the Everton team who played against Glasgow Rangers in an FA Cup tie. The game, already surrendered by the Anfield club, resulted in a 1-0 win for the Scotsmen. Next season, along with five of his fellow countrymen, he took part in the famous FA Cup marathon against Bolton Wanderers. Everton, at the fourth attempt, won the tie but were then found guilty of making "illegal payments" to their players and banned from taking part in next year's tournament. Everton then registered Sandy as a professional and he took in their inaugural Football League season. However, as Everton had signed Nick Ross, he played only nine league games before ending his career in the reserve side. When Everton decamped and moved to Goodison Park, Sandy remained at Anfield and took over the training duties with the new Liverpool Football Club. He also managed a public house at 41 Whitefield Road in Everton.

Sandy later worked on the catering staff at the Liverpool Cotton Exchange until, after suffering a long and painful illness, he died at the age of 60. He left a wife and three children. Sandy Dick, at the time of his death, was living at 271 County Road, Walton and his funeral, which was well attended, took place at Anfield cemetery. Mr J Fare represented the Everton directors while W H Parry, Andrew Gibson and J W Platt paid their last respects on behalf of the former players.

James Cassidy arrived, without ceremony, at Everton in September 1887 and played a part in the epic FA Cup tie with Bolton Wanderers. Little is known of his previous activity but it is distinctly possible that he was a promising young teenage winger who came to Liverpool from the Kilmarnock area. He lost his place in the Everton team when summonsed before the FA tribune at the Crompton Hotel in Liverpool. He went back home to play for Kilmarnock before returning to England where he enjoyed a long career with his old adversaries, Bolton Wanderers.

John Goudie was another of the several experienced Scottish players who were engaged by the Everton directors in the hope of quickly closing the gap that existed between their club and those representing the mill towns of Lancashire. He was born in 1860 at 49 High Street in Paisley. Goudie came to Everton from the Abercorn club who were based in Paisley at Underwood Park. He had previously won one International cap, 26 1 1884, when he scored for Scotland in a 5-0 win over Ireland on the Ballyneifiegh ground in Belfast. John Goudie arrived in Liverpool at the beginning of the season and scored twice on his debut against Bury after Anfield. He then played a full part in the four game FA Cup struggle with Bolton Wanderers and scored one of the goals that finally won the tie in favour of Everton. John Goudie also took part in the FA Cup defeat at Preston and then left Everton after his amateur status what brought into question. He later played, along with other members of his family, for Kilmarnock Athletic.

John Weir was a halfback who played his football with Third Lanark before moving south where, after playing with Preston North End, he first played for Bootle in September 1887. He had previously won one International cap when he represented Scotland, 19 2 1887, against Ireland at Hampden Park. Weir had been on Merseyside for about eight weeks when he was involved in a controversial incident that was to cause a rift between Everton and their neighbours at Hawthorne Road. The Scot, it had been announced, was to appear for Bootle in an FA Cup tie against Workington but at the eleventh hour, he decided instead to travel with Everton on the occasion of their FA Cup tie against Bolton Wanderers at Pikes Lane. Everton, at the fourth attempt, eventually won the tie. John Weir, following a protest from Bolton, was called before an FA tribunal, held in Star Chamber fashion, at the Crompton Hotel in Liverpool where the regional officials questioned him concerning his amateur status. Everton Football Club had been accused of paying certain players who were on their register as amateurs thus breaking rules that governed the National knockout. The Scot claimed he had always been an amateur football player and escaped with a caution. John Weir later signed professional forms with Everton and represented them in 16 matches during their initial season as members of the Football League. Next season, on his third outing, he fell awkwardly and broke his arm in the match against Wolverhampton Wanderers and never played first team football for Everton again.

Robert Izzat was first reported to be playing on Merseyside, with Bootle, in December 1886. He is thought to have developed a friendship with John Weir when he suddenly left Bootle and threw in "his lot" with Everton. A Lancashire sports paper had this to say on the occasion…*Bootle and Everton have long been at open feud and their relations are now of a most bitter character. It was announced in all the Liverpool journals that the Bootle team would include two players – Izatt and Weir – in the FA Cup tie against Workington. The personnel of the Everton side in the tie with the Wanderers at Bolton was kept a profound secret until their appearance at Pikes Lane. These two facts, taken in conjunction would appear to indicate that the secession of Izatt and Weir was effected in a manner such as to call forth the reprobation of all* *fair dealing men. The question is of course not for us to discuss. The players are amateurs, and can carry their services to the most congenial quarters. But I do not think that such action as theirs, in leaving their late club to commence an important Cup tie short handed, can be too strongly characterized, no notice whatsoever of their intention having been purveyed to the Bootle authorities, while it would appear that every possible means were adopted to keep them in ignorance of the fact. As to the event itself, no surprise whatsoever has been felt at the action of Izatt, who has long been intractable, and Bootle have little cause to be aggravated by the loss of Weir. This Scotch amateur has now been in the Liverpool district for some two months, and has passed through the ranks of the three leadings clubs. He will be a distinct gain to Everton, but It is very improbable that Izzat will long retain a position in the Anfield Road eleven, and he has evidently only been accepted as an inseparable of Weir. (The Football Field)* Nevertheless Izatt took part in all four FA Cup ties with Bolton Wanderers while John Weir was selected to play in just one. He was then called to give evidence at the FA tribunal and never played football for Everton again.

Robert Watson had, prior to joining Everton; previously played football with the Thistle club in Glasgow and is first seen on Merseyside, 11 4 1887, when he played for them against Bootle at Hawthorne Road. It is likely, but difficult to ascertain, that this is the time that the Everton directors first approached Rob Watson for he later made his Everton debut, 8 10 1887, against Notts County on Trent Bridge Cricket Ground. Next Saturday Rob Watson took part in an FA Cup and scored one of the goals for Everton as they drew 2-2 with Bolton Wanderers at Pikes Lane. He took part in all four of the FA Cup ties that were required to eliminate Bolton Wanderers and also in the 2nd round tie against Preston North End. He was then one of the seven players deemed to be of "professional status" and was forced to leave Everton but returned, as a professional, at the beginning of next season. He played 18 games in the clubs inaugural Football League season and scored 4 goals. However, the Everton forward line had managed only 35 goals and the directorate did not retain Watson who left to join Gorton Villa in Manchester. His former club, Glasgow Thistle became, in 1893, founder members of the Scottish Division Two but folded one year later.

Nick Ross was reported to be the country's highest paid football player when, in the summer of 1888; he agreed to join Everton for a wage of £10 per week. He was born, December 1862, in Edinburgh and began playing football with a side called Hanover who he captained at the age of 18. One year later he joined Heart of Midlothian. In 1882 he was selected to play for Scotland against England, but an accident prevented him from taking part in the encounter. He was captain of Hearts when, in 1883, they lifted the local Roseberry trophy before a further injury again prevented him from representing Scotland. In July 1883 he proceeded to Preston (at the invitation of Mr. T McNeil) where he worked at his trade as a flagger and slater. He began to play football for North End when the season commenced but he returned to Edinburgh the following year where, on the occasion of his wedding, he received a large gratuity from the Hearts of Midlothian directors. Ross returned to Preston where he played on the left wing until an accident to one of the fullbacks necessitated his appearance in that position. Nick Ross was enjoying his new roll when he left Preston North End and transferred to Everton.

The appearance of Nick Ross in Liverpool caused a stir among the local football fans and around three thousand turned up to watch a pre-season kick about on Belmont Road. The Everton executive was then hoping to include Ross in the opening game of the season, against Padiham, but his clearance had not yet come through from the FA. However, with 15 minutes to spare, a telegraph, sent by Charles Alcock, arrived at the Sandon Hotel giving the Scot the "all clear". Nick Ross immediately accepted the Everton captaincy and held the position until his departure at the end of the season. He began the season playing a full back but was soon under pressure to play a more forward role in the hope of solving the club's goal scoring problems. Ross did not appear to enjoy playing among the forwards preferring instead to play, as he did at Preston, at full back. There was, however, a certain incident, reported in the *Liverpool Courier*, which could also have given him reason to leave Everton and rejoin his younger brother at Preston.

Sir.

During the progress of and since the match West Bromwich Albion v Everton of Saturday last, I have heard many hard things said of N.J. Ross, the captain of the Everton first team, of his play in the above game. I myself did not consider he was doing as well as expected but under the circumstances that I have been assured of, and coming from a source I have no reason to doubt, I take this matter before the public, the chief supporter of the last mentioned club. The facts are as follows...the visiting team at once objected to the globe placed on the field for hostilities, on the grounds that it was not true; therefore appealed to captain of the home team for new ball, and he in turn, as was his duty, appealed to one of the leading spirits of the management committee in the person of one of the management, for his aforesaid article and was immediately snubbed in the following terms "mind your own business and go to your place. All you are required to do is play the game". Now I maintain that such a speech was quite uncalled for before an audience of football members. Such treatment of a first class player is sufficient to be most careful in giving him content to play for the Everton club. (Liverpool Courier 28 February, 1889.)

Nick Ross did not play in the one remaining Everton league fixture, against Blackburn Rovers, but he did take part in several friendly matches that were arranged to see the club through to the end of the season. He and his family then left Liverpool and resettled off

Avenham Lane in Preston. Ross resigned for Preston North End and next season led them to the football league championship. He wore the Preston colours until 1893 when ill health forced him to retire from the game. Nick Ross, with a view to recuperating, spent a considerable amount of time on the Fylde coast and also took a voyage to the Canary Islands. The Scot, in the hope of regaining his health, took a cottage on Longridge Fells but did not survive to enjoy the benefit of its location. In November 1894, Nick Ross took to his bed at his residence (34 Berry Street) but, after treatment, was able get up and move above the house. He appeared, for a while, to make a slight recovery but then suddenly got worse and quickly died. Nicholas John Ross had touched the hearts of everybody in Preston and his sudden death was the one sole topic of conversation amongst his many friends and admirers. The streets were lined with mourners as his funeral cortège passed through the town on the way to Preston Cemetery and there were closed shutters and drawn blinds on all sides testifying to the high regard in which Ross was held among all sections of the community. The directors of the local football club were among the two hundred or so people who filled the mortuary chapel to hear the simple service. Several of his former teammates carried his coffin from the chapel to its last resting place. Nick Ross was survived by his wife and five children.

Hugh Pollock was born at New Milns, Ayrshire in 1867. He began playing football with Kilmarnock Athletic from where, along with Sandy Dick, he moved south to play his football with Liverpool Stanley. On the 29th of September 1888, he stood in for the injured Jonny Holt against Bolton Wanderers at Pikes Lane. It was Hugh Pollock's one and only league match for Everton.

Rob Stephenson accompanied Sandy Dick and Hugh Pollock on the Exodus from Kilmarnock to the Stanley Football Club in Liverpool. He was of "amateur status" which enabled him to assist the team of his choice if required to do so. Stephenson, when requested, took part in one league game for Everton, a 5-0 defeat away at Wolverhampton, before returning to play for Stanley.

Archibald McKinnon was the first player to score a hat trick for Everton in a football League match and he did so on the 27th of October, against Derby County at Anfield. He was born, 1864, at 24 Dean Street, Edinburgh and was playing with his local club, St Bernard's, just prior to joining Everton. McKinnon, during his short stay with Everton, played in 7 league matches and scored 4 goals. His late arrival was the reason he missed the opening game with Accrington and he first tested the Anfield turf when he represented Everton in a friendly match against Liverpool Stanley. McKinnon made his Football League debut, playing at centre half, in the club's second league match against Notts County. The Scot, it was reported, was then sent back North of the Tweed to search for suitable players but the people he suggested do not appear to have found favour with the Everton board. McKinnon played his last game for Everton, 3 11 1888, against Bolton Wanderers and then promptly returned to Scotland. His sudden departure however, did not go unnoticed in Scotland...*McKinnon has returned to Edinburgh because the Everton club would not do anything more to find him a good situation. He wanted payment and when they refused to give him anything he left the team in the lurch, but luckily there was reserve team man along, and his services were utilsed. This is Scotch amateurism.* (Scottish Sport 23rd November 1888.) The following passage, from the Everton minute book, confirms his prompt departure...*after considerable discussion as to the in and out performance of the 1st team and also McKinnon's defection it was agreed to adjourn the meeting.* 12 11 1888. McKinnon returned to Edinburgh where he spent the rest of his career playing football for Heart of Midlothian.

John Coyne was reported to have come to Everton from Gainsborough Trinity having previously played his football in Scotland with the Vale of Leven. He went straight in to the first eleven and scored on his debut, 24 11 1888, in a 3-2 win over Burnley at Anfield. Coyne then made his second, and final, league appearance against West Bromwich Albion at Stoney Lane and did not play for Everton again.

George Davie also made two leagues appearances for Everton and came from the same part of Scotland as John Coyne. On the 2 4 1888 he is reported as playing for Renton against Vale of Leven in the local County cup final at Boghead Park in Dumbarton. One week later he is seen in Lancashire playing for Renton against Burnley at Turf Moor. George Davie then made his Everton debut, 24 11 1888, against Burnley at Anfield. The following Saturday he represented Everton against West Bromwich Albion and never appeared for the club again. George Davie later moved to London where he played football for Royal Arsenal and represented the Gunners in four FA Cup ties.

John William Angus was given a trial period by the Everton directorate in the hope he would help to alleviate the problem the club was then experiencing with scoring goals. He was born 1 12 1868; on New Road in Blytheswood, a once populated area of central Glasgow, now given over to commerce, just off Sauchiehall Street. Angus is first seen in Everton colours, 11 12 1888, playing in a friendly match against Burslam Port Vale on the Staffordshire club's ground at Colebridge before making his league debut, 22 12 1888, against Preston North End at Deepdale. On Boxing Day he played for Everton against Bootle before a crowd of over 16,000 at Goodison Park and was then selected to play in the forthcoming game against Blackburn Rovers. However, the surface of the Anfield was affected by the cold weather and deemed unfit to stage a league fixture so the game was declared to be friendly. Next Saturday Angus took to the field with Everton in a league fixture against Accrington on the Thornyholme Ground. The visitors, who arrived a man short, were forced to enlist the services of H. Parkinson, an amateur with a local club who played under the name of Bells Temperance. Jack Angus then played in the next 3 league games for Everton before being dropped without scoring a goal. He remained in the reserve side for the rest of season and last played for the senior eleven, 21 4 1888, in a club fixture against the Scottish Cup holders, Renton before being released by Everton at the end of the season.

John Angus then moved to Manchester where he played football with Ardwick before moving south to join Southampton St Mary's.

Andrew Hannah was the first of four top-notch Scottish football players who arrived at Anfield during the summer of 1889. He was born, 17 9 1864, in the town of Renton and had previously won two Scottish Cup winners' medals with his local club. Playing at full back, Hannah had also represented Scotland in their 5-1 win over Wales at Edinburgh in 1888. The Scot had previously joined West Bromwich Albion but, having failed to settle in the Midlands, returned to his former home in the Vale of Leven. On the 23 4 1889 Andrew Hannah arrived at Anfield with the Renton team to play a fixture against Everton and it seemed he agreed, there and then, to join Everton.

Hannah made his Everton debut, 7 9 1889, in a 3-2 home win over Blackburn Rovers and played in all 22 football league matches in his inaugural season with Everton. Next season, having missed just two matches, he captained Everton to their first ever Football League championship. However, for some unknown reason, he decided to return to Scotland where he re-joined his former club Renton. Andrew Hannah had played in 42 league and cup games for Everton.

John Houlding later persuaded the Scot to return to Merseyside and captain his newly formed Liverpool FC. Andrew Hannah remained at Anfield for three seasons before ending his career with Rob Roy Kirkintilloch.

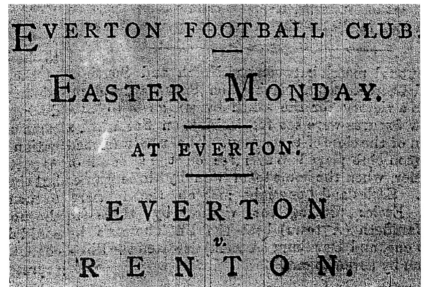

Daniel Doyle was signed to play at full back and along with Andy Hannah and together they formed a formidable barrier in front of the Everton goal. (Both players shared the same birthday.) He was just less than six foot tall and weighed over twelve stone. Doyle was born into a poor Irish family at Paisley where he lost his father at the age of 6. In 1871 he is reported to be living with his aunt and uncle in Airdrie while in 1881, he is reported to be working as a coal miner while still living in Airdrie.

He began his football career with Rawyard Juniors before moving to play for Broxburn Shamrocks in West Lothian. The talents of Doyle seemed to have alerted the Hibernian executive because in 1888 he is reported to be playing for the Edinburgh Club. In 1889 Doyle has somehow been enticed to join Grimsby Town where he was involved in the first football fatality. The match was against Staveley and it took place on the home of the Grimsby club at Clee Park. Doyle collided with William Cropper and accidentally caught him in the stomach causing a painful injury. The Staveley player was carried to the dressing room where he died, the next day, from peritonitis. Danny Doyle, following the incident, moved onto Lancashire where he signed for Bolton Wanderers.

On 6 4 1890 he played for Bolton Wanderers against Everton in a match which took place at Anfield that was designed to raise money for Stanley Hospital. Doyle later signed for Everton and moved to Liverpool. The club executive placed him under the care of Mrs. Hughes who ran a boarding house at 26 Coniston Street. He was ever present in the 1889-90 football season and scored one goal in an FA Cup tie that was played against Derby County at Anfield. He was also part of the 1891 championship winning side. Danny Doyle played 42 league and cup games for Everton before leaving the club in controversial circumstances.

On the 11 9 1891 news reached Liverpool that Danny Doyle, along with another Everton player, had been spotted playing football for Celtic FC against Cowlairs in Glasgow. The two players would now not be eligible to represent Everton in the forthcoming F.A.Cup tournament. The Anfield club had no hold over Brady but Doyle was under contract until 30 4 1893. Furthermore, he had left his lodgings in Liverpool and was now residing at Marlborough Street in Glasgow. Everton however, claimed to have already paid Doyle for his future services and decided they would go through the legal process of reclaiming their money. On 16 January 1892, the two parties met at the Sheriffs Court in Glasgow.

Richard Molyneux, who appeared on behave of Everton, told the court that the terms set out in the contract, relating to Daniel Doyle, were that … "the player to receive £91 on the 1ST of May 1891 and that his out of his season wages were to be 25s per week during the rest of the 1891/92 season. The terms of agreement, as modified by he club, were that, on 30th May 1891 the defender is paid £15 and, on 18th August 1891, he had received a further £15". Danny Doyle told the court that the reason he terminated his contract was that the Celtic club was nearer to his home in Airdrie. He stated that he had served Everton for 14 weeks for wages that accounted to £42 and was willing to return the balance, which amounted to £69, back to the club. Everton won the case but lost a first class football player.

Danny Doyle reclaimed his amateur status and pursued the rest of his football career with the Celtic club and became a great favourite with their supporters. Later, his playing days over, he ran a Whisky distillery. However, towards the end of his life, he had fallen on hard times while suffering from ill health. Danny Doyle, after a painful illness, died in Glasgow where he was buried. He was 53.

Alexander Brady was born, 2 4 1865 and learnt his football with Renton Juniors before crossing the border to join Sunderland as an amateur. In 1888 he moved to Burnley where he represented the Turf Moor Club during their first season in the Football League. In 1889 he appeared to have agreed professional terms with the Turf Moor club before accepting an improved offer to join Everton. However, the FA did not take kindly to his actions and issued him with a short suspension that caused a delay to his league debut with Everton.

The club executive, meanwhile, had lodged Brady, along with Doyle and Hannah, at the home of Mrs. Hughes in Coniston Street. He made his Everton debut 2 11 1889, and scored twice in an 8-0 home win over Stoke. Brady later made his FA Cup debut at home against Derby County and scored a hat trick in the 11-2 win. (This remains the record victory for Everton). Next season he re-signed for Everton and missed only one league match as he scored 9 goals to help Everton win the league championship. Alec Brady played 34 league games and scored 17 goals before, along with Danny Doyle, he left the club and signed amateur forms with Celtic.

Nevertheless, he did not stay long with the Glasgow club and soon drifted away back to England. Alec Brady eventually settled in Yorkshire where he had a prolonged spell with The Wednesday club in Sheffield. He played 158 league games with south Yorkshire club and was part of the side that, in 1898, won the FA Cup.

Alex Latta joined Everton from Dumbarton Athletic just prior to their amalgamation with neighbours Dumbarton. He was born,

7 9 1863 at 45 Church Street Dumbarton to John Latta, a local journeyman shipwright and his Falkirk born wife, Margaret. He was a powerfully built man who was described as being "as modest as he is accomplished". Latta won two caps for Scotland the first of which was against Wales in 1888. On 13th April 1889 he won his second cap when he played against England at the Oval Cricket Ground in London. He then sacrificed his International career by signing professional forms with Everton.

A. LATTA (Dumbarton Athletic F.C.

Latta made his debut, against Blackburn Rovers, on the opening day of the season and soon picked up the pact of the game in England. He scored his first goal at Bolton 4 weeks later. Latta missed just three league games during his first campaign as Everton finished runners up to Preston North End. Next season he was injured while playing for the Lancashire F.A. and completed just 10 league games during Everton's first championship season. The following season Latta was the club's leading scorer with 17 goals. On 19th October 1892 he scored all four goals as Everton won 4-3 away against Newton Heath in Manchester. Alex Latta spent 6 seasons with Everton taking part in 148 league and cup games and scoring 70 goals. Alex Latta then set up a boat building business at 13 Banks Road, Hoylake and occasionally, he would play football for Rock Ferry. He later went bankrupt took a job with the Rutherford shipping building company. Alex Latta died 25 8 1925.

Walter "Willie" Cox had enjoyed a long career with his local club Hibernian where he always played among the forwards. From as early as 1879 he is reported to be being for the Edinburgh club and last represented them, against Renton, in the 1886 semi-final of the Scottish Cup. Willie then decided to try his luck in England where he signed for Burnley. Asked to play in goal by the Turf Moor executive he took kindly to his new role and made the position his own. However, after a series of heavy defeats, he left Burnley in January 1890 and returned to his home in Leith. Four weeks later, Everton were knocking on his door.

Richard Molyneux, the then secretary of Everton, travelled to Edinburgh and signed the Scot at his home. He then caught the train to London to register his papers with the FA. Two days later Mr. Molyneux attended a local meeting of the Football League and, with all items legitimate, Willie Cox was clear to play in England. He first played for Everton in a reserve fixture against Blackpool based South Shore at Anfield. Two weeks later he represented the first eleven in a home fixture against Glasgow Rangers. It was the first time the Scottish club had appeared at Anfield since their famous FA Cup tie of 1886 when Everton, having forfeited the game, had lost by 1 goal to 0. This time, things were very different. Willie Cox, who was seldom troubled in the game and looked on as Everton, with pulsating performance, routed the visitors by 8 goals to 1. Next Saturday he made his Football League debut, 22 2 1890, on the Thornyholme Ground against Accrington. Everton, who lost 5-3, were reported to be the victims of a couple of rather dubious decisions made by the match officials. Willie Cox then kept goal in the three remaining league fixtures as Everton narrowly missed out on the league title that was won by Preston North End. The season however, was far from over.

Willie Cox was a member of the Everton party who visited Scotland when all the football league fixtures had been completed. The large crowd, who assembled to see their favourites off, voiced their concern when three members of squad were not on board when the train left the Station. It later transpired that the three players, namely, Hammond, Holt and Millward, had mistaken the time of departure but, after taking the next train, they arrived in time to join the Everton party as they settled down for the night at the George Hotel in Glasgow. The demands of hospitality were duly honoured by the hosts who treated their guests, immediately after breakfast, to a three-hour sail down the River Clyde arriving back with plenty of time to prepare for the game. The match was played on the new home of the Rangers club at Govan and it attracted a crowd of over 4,000 people. The home club was anxious to avoid another heavy defeat and they had strengthened their team with Fraser from St Mirren and Allen and Jon McPherson of Cowlairs. All three players contributed to a game in which Willie Cox was outstanding. He made several good saves and helped Everton to a 6-2 victory. The home goalkeeper, a player named Reid, does not appear to have played as well as his Everton counterpart. A Liverpool journalist, who accompanied the Everton team, had this

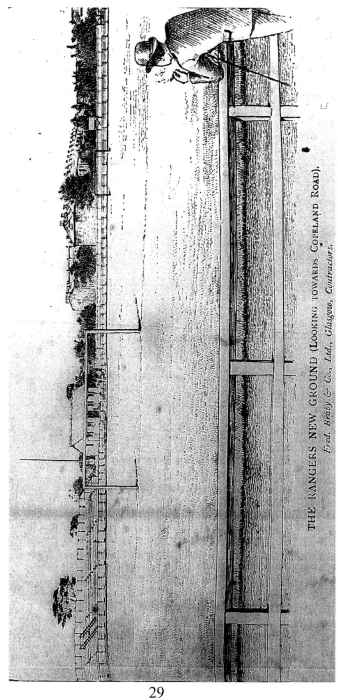

THE RANGERS NEW GROUND (LOOKING TOWARDS COPELAND ROAD).

Fred. Braby & Co., Ltd., Glasgow, Contractors.

to say...*there was only one weakness in the home side, and that was at goal. Reid being very feeble, in striking contrast to Cox, who behaved splendidly in goal, and gave Everton more faith in him, his display doing much to retrieve his recent failures. (Liverpool Mercury 21 4 1890.)* Next morning the Everton party took a ride out to Dumbarton and returned to catch their train from Glasgow. They alighted at Carlisle where they spent the night before continuing on to play a match with Sunderland. Willie Cox, who played in goal, could not prevent Everton from losing by 3 goals to 2. He then played several friendly games before leaving Everton, during the summer, to join Nottingham Forest.

John Angus came to Everton from Sunderland Albion and was part of the squad that first brought the league championship to Anfield. He was born in the small Aberdeenshire town of King Edward before moving, with his parents, to the town of Dennyloanhead in Stirlingshire. John Angus, after leaving school, trained to be a plumber and gas fitter while also keeping goal for the nearby Kings Park FC in the town of Sterling. He then left Scotland and spent three seasons with Sunderland Albion before leaving the Wearside club when their application to join the Football League was turned down. John Angus next joined Everton.

The young Scotsman made his debut in a holiday fixture against Bootle on Whit Monday 1890. He was featured in the Everton goal when they began the season with a 4-1 win against West Bromwich Albion at the Hawthorns. Angus made another ten league appearances before losing his place to Dave Jardine who had recently joined the club from Bootle. His last senior appearance, when Jardine was ineligible, was in an FA Cup tie at Sunderland in January 1890. Angus kept goal for the second eleven until, at the end of the season, he returned home to his parents in Denny. There he contracted Typhoid Fever and was confined to his bed. John Angus died, aged 25, on 8th August and was buried in the local cemetery. He was unmarried.

Walter Campbell was born, circa 1867, and appears on the 1871 census living with his parents in the lowland town of Moffat. His father, Walter senior, is listed as being a stonemason. In 1891 the family had moved to Bootle and are were living at 26 Clare Road. "Wattie" Campbell now 23 is listed as an apprentice engine fitter. In 1888 he is reported to be playing football for Bootle. Campbell had had previous trials with Everton but they had not proved successful. However, following a great improvement in his play, it was announced, in March 1890, that he would soon be leaving Bootle to join Everton. "Wattie" was a popular wee character with the Hawthorne Road faithfully who, for his last few remaining games,

Wattie Campbell (back row, second from the right) is seen here with the Bootle team prior to his move to Everton. Tam Vietch, also in the picture, stands to the right of the trophy.

aired their displeasure when they learnt of his decision to leave the Bootle club and assist their main rivals Everton. Walter Campbell made his football league debut for Everton in the opening match of 1889/90 season and scored in a 4-1 win over West Bromwich Albion at the Hawthorns. He played another 13 league games for Everton to help them to win the championship in 1891. "Wattie"

Campbell played another 4 league games before dropping down to the Combination side. In July 1893 his family was in the news when a certain William Campbell fell to his death during the construction of Blackpool Tower. The story appeared in several Northern newspapers...*On Wednesday morning, William Campbell, labourer, of Liverpool, brother to Campbell of Everton football fame, fell from the tower at Blackpool, which has now reached a height of 400foot, and was killed immediately. (The Huddersfield Chronicle, 11 7 1893.)* The man who lost his life was in fact the cousin of Walter and not his brother. Nevertheless his death, watched by a large holiday crowd, was a tragedy.

David Jardine was born, 5 12 1865, in the small Dumfrieshire village Templand, near Lochmaben, where his father worked as a stonemason. He began his football career by keeping goal for Mid Annandale FC, who was based at nearby Lockerbie, and it was from there that he joined Bootle in 1888. His outstanding displays soon attracted the attentions of the Everton directorate who secured his signature in November 1890. The Anfield club paid Bootle £75 for the transfer while Jardine himself received a fee of £20. He made his debut four weeks later at Wolverhampton, when Jack Angus was indisposed through illness. He proved a reliable deputy and was part of the Everton side that secured the League championship at Turf Moor in March 1890. He shared the goal keeping duties with Williams and was between the posts when Everton played Nottingham Forest in the first Football League match to be played at Goodison Park. Dave Jardine made 37 league appearances for Everton before leaving to join the Lancashire League side, Nelson from where he later played for Wrexham.

Robert Cain was signed from Airdrieonians as a possible replacement for George Farmer and made his debut, 2 11 1889; in the 8-0 home win over Stoke. He was described as a strong tackling half back who could use his weight to good effect. Cain was born 13 2 1866 at Slamannan. He played 10 league games for Everton before leaving to join Bootle at the end of the season. He played one season at Hawthorne Road before accepting an invitation to sign for Sheffield United. Bob Cain proved to be a sound investment for the Yorkshire side playing for them in over 170 league and FA Cup games. He later played Southern League football with Tottenham Hotspur before ending his career with Albion Rovers.

Hope Robertson played 29 league games for Everton and scored one goal. He was born, 17 1 1866, at Whiteinch (now part of Glasgow) and began playing football with junior side, Minerva. He served his time as a boilermaker and joined Partick Thistle in August 1889. He played three games for the Jags before moving to London where he assisted Woolwich Arsenal in their inaugural F.A. Cup campaign. He made his debut on the Woolwich Arsenal ground at Plumstead and scored twice as the Gunners beat Lyndhurst by 11 goals to 1. Robertson played another three games the Gunners, scoring twice in process, before leaving to rejoin Partick Thistle following their elimination from the tournament by the Swifts.

Andrew Hannah, during a visit to Scotland, persuaded Robertson to come down and join Everton where he received a signing on fee of £50 that was followed by a wage of £3,10s a week. He made his Everton debut, 8 11 1890, at Blackburn. The following week, on his home debut, he scored the only goal of the game that secured two points for Everton at the expense of Sunderland. In 1891 Hope Robertson is reported as living at 41 Bulwer Street, Everton with his Liverpool born wife Elizabeth. He was later tried at halfback but, having lost favour with the selectors, accepted an invitation to join Bootle in November 1893. He played ten Football League games for the north Merseyside club before leaving them, at the end of the season, when they went into liquidation. He returned to Partick Thistle where he made 27 appearances and scored two goals in 1894 before he returned to England and played ten games for Walsall Town Swifts. Hope Robertson then returned to Scotland where he ended his career with Airdrieonians.

Robert Jamieson joined Bootle from Dumbarton having previously represented the Sons of the Rock in the 1886/87 Scottish cup final against Hibernian. He made his debut for the Hawthorne Road side in a 1-0 victory over Newton Heath in January 1888. While at Bootle he joined the Merchant Navy and was not always available for selection. He played one league match as an amateur, for Everton, 15 3 1890, and assisted them in a 3-1 win over Derby County. Pushed in to a right wing position he looked all at sea in unfamiliar waters but his contribution was sufficient to ensure a victory. He later signed professional forms preferring to play second team football with Everton as opposed to first team football at Bootle.

Alexander Lochhead was born, 27 2 1866, in the Renfrewshire town of Johnston. He played football for both Lugar and Arthurlie before joining Third Lanark who he represented in the 1889 Scottish Cup Final, at Hampden Park against Glasgow Celtic. The Thirds won the match, played in a snowstorm, by 2 goals to 1. However, following a Celtic protest, the SFA ordered the game to be re-played on the same venue. Third Lanark, clearly miffed by the proceedings, again demonstrated their superiority over their opponents by beating them by 3 goals to 0. Alex Lochhead won his only cap for Scotland when, along with five of his Third Lanark teammates, he took part in the 0-0 draw against Wales on the Racecourse Ground at Wrexham. In February 1890, he signed professional forms with Everton.

Alex Lochhead received a payment of £130 and accepted a wage of £3 a week. He made his Everton debut, for the second eleven, in a 6-1 win away at Walsall Town Swifts before taking part in the championship deciding match, against Burnley, at Turf Moor. The match was played on a pitch that was nothing more then a sea of mud and water and the young Scotsman, who struggled with the pace of game, was glad of the assistance of Danny Doyle. Everton appeared to have had the game won until, with 2 late goals, Burnley appeared to have wrenched the championship away from them. Nevertheless, Preston North End, who had to win at Sunderland, also lost so the championship belonged to Everton. Alex Lochhead played another 5 league games for Everton before returning to Third Lanark from where he ended his playing career with Clyde.

Daniel Kirkwood was born in the shale mining town of Broxburn, West Lothian where he played local football before joining the East Stirlingshire club at nearby Falkirk. In 1889 he accepted the offer to play for Everton. Danny Kirkwood quickly bedded in to a stylish half back line that also included John Holt and Walter Campbell, and was part of the Everton side that won the league championship. Next season he left Anfield and helped to form the Liverpool Caledonian club where a bad injury finally put paid to his playing career. Kirkwood married a local girl and settled in Liverpool where he ran a newsagents shop on Townsend Lane. He continued to maintain close links with Everton FC and later became a director of the club's while also taking charge of coaching the young players at the club's training ground in Fazakerley. Daniel Kirkwood was a canny Scot and a successful businessman who later ran both a public house and a Chandlers shop at 58 Priory Road, Liverpool. He retired to Wirral where he died, 23 12 1928, whilst living at 4 Trafalgar Road in Wallesey and was survived by his wife, Charlotte.

Duncan MacLean began playing junior football with Renton before stepping up to play with the senior side in the town. He was born, 1869, in the town of Alexandra and was 20 years old when he joined his former teammate, Andrew Hannah, at Anfield. McLean was immediately placed under the care of Mrs. Evans at her home in Coniston Street. He made his Everton debut against Blackburn Rovers and played 6 league and F.A. Cup matches during the 1890/91 championship season. Next season he established himself in the Everton side and appeared in 20 league matches. MacLean decided to continue playing his football at Anfield, when Everton left for Goodison Park, where he was again re-united with his former skipper, Andrew Hannah. He remained at Anfield until October 1896 when he returned to Scotland to play for the St Bernard's club in Edinburgh. He later won 2 caps for Scotland the first of which occurred, 23 3 1896, at the Port Carolina ground in Dundee.

Patrick Gordon came to Everton along with Duncan MacLean and also lodged at the home of Mrs. Evans. He was born, 1864, in Renton where he began playing for his local club. Everton gave Gordon a baptism of fire when he made his debut, 22 11 1890, away against the all-conquering Preston North End with whom Everton were engaged in the struggle for the league championship. Preston won the game by 2 goals to 0. Nevertheless, Gordon played in the two remaining league games that saw Everton through to the championship. The Scot had joined Everton at a time when the competition for first team places was at a premium and he played only four league games during the season that followed.

He then played eleven league games during Everton's last season at Anfield and scored one goal. However, Pat Gordon also played his part in helping the club to reach their first ever FA Cup Final by scoring twice in the three match semi-final battle with Preston North End. He was then a member of the side beaten by Wolverhampton Wanderers, in the final at Fallowfield in Manchester. The club directors then gave a free transfer to Gordon who chose to remain at Anfield and play for Liverpool when Everton left the location. He later played football for both Blackburn Rovers and Wigan County before ending his career with Liverpool South End. Patrick Gordon married a Liverpool girl with whom he raised a family. He lived at 306 Netherfield Road and was employed as a dock labourer.

Thomas B Wyllie was the first player to be signed by Everton from Glasgow Rangers. He received a £100 signing on fee and accepted a wage of £3 a week.
This was, at the time, considered to be excessive but the Anfield

club desperately needed a class player to replace the injured Alex Latta. Wylie had previously made one appearance for Scotland, 29 3 1889, scoring in a 4-1 win over Ireland in Belfast. He was born, 1872, in the Ayrshire town of Maybole from where, in the summer of 1888, he accepted the invitation to play for Glasgow Rangers. Wylie had been 2 seasons with the Ibrox club and was part of the team who took part in their inaugural season in the Scottish Football League. He played 4 league games for Rangers before joining Everton in November 1889.

Wylie was given rather abrupt introduction to English football when he made his Everton debut away at Wolverhampton Wanderers. There was a crowd of 12,000 assembled at the Molineux Grounds when Everton took to the field wearing their new their new colours of blue and gold stripes. Wylie, who played at outside right, helped Everton to win the game with a single goal that was scored by Geary. The result, sent home by telegraph, was joyfully received when it was posted on the window of the several newspaper offices in Liverpool. However, the mood soon changed when a further newspaper reached the streets of Liverpool some hours later. A gang of ruffians, it was reported, had attacked the Everton players as they were leaving the field but it did not say if any of them had been hurt.

The news of such an outrage caused anger amongst the large number of local football followers who had gathered at Lime Street Station when the Everton party arrived back home. They were all delighted to discover that their favourites, Tom Wylie amongst them, had all escaped unscathed. Next Saturday the Scot made his home debut and scored a hat trick in a 6-2 win over Derby County. Wylie, who played the next two games, then helped Everton to win the league championship. Next season he played 16 league games but scored only one goal as Everton completed their final season at Anfield before they moved to Goodison Park. Tom Wylie was one of several players who chose to remain at Anfield to play

Lancashire League football with the newly formed Liverpool Club. He later joined Bury before ending his playing days, as an amateur, with Bristol City.

Jack Elliott was first seen at Goodison Park when he appeared in the ranks of Battlefield FC from Glasgow and scored two goals in a match against the Everton second eleven. He then joined Partick Thistle from where he made a permanent move to Everton in November 1890. Elliott was set to make his debut, 1 11 1890, in a second XI match against Earlestown but was suddenly ordered to take an express train to Nottingham because he was needed to replace Alex Latta who had been suddenly taken ill. He arrived just in time to take the field at Trent Bridge and took part in the league game against Notts County. He then spent the rest of the season playing for the reserve side. Jack Elliott remained at Everton for five seasons making 15 league appearances and scoring one goal, 18 3 1893, against Wolverhampton Wanderers. In 1896 he was not retained as player and returned to Scotland before returning, several years later to fill the position as club trainer with everton. In 1911 Jack Elliott is reported to be living at 42 Naseby Road where he gives his occupation as a football trainer. With him are his wife and five children the two oldest of which had been born in Scotland. In 1936 Jack Elliott gives an interview to the *Liverpool Echo* and tells them he had worked all his life for Everton Football Club filling the roll of both trainer and groundsman. He died, 12 9 1940, at 1 Oban Road in Liverpool.

Abraham Hartley came to Everton from Dumbarton where he had been born in 1871. He began his career, along with other members of his family, playing junior football for Artizan Thistle before joining the town's senior club at Boghead Park. Hartley was part of the Dumbarton squad who shared the inaugural Scottish league championship with Rangers and he also helped them to win the title outright one year later. In 1892 he decided to follow his former teammate Rob Kelso over the border to Everton.

Hartley arrived in Liverpool at Christmas time and took part in the local derby game, played against Bootle, at Goodison Park. He quickly endeared himself to 16,000 spectators by scoring for Everton in a 1-1 draw. Abe spent some time with the Everton Combination side before scoring against Wolves on his first team debut at Molineux. Hartley spent another five seasons at Goodison scoring 24 goals in 50 league matches. His most cherished moments however, came in the FA Cup. Hartley scored one of the goals that helped Everton beat Derby County by 3 goals to 2 in the semi-final to set up a final tie with Aston Villa. He then took part in the 1897 FA Cup final played at the Crystal Palace but could not prevent Everton from losing by 3 goals to 2. Next season was to be Abe Hartley's last with Everton. He began the campaign well by scoring, 18 9 1897, a hat trick against Wolves but then failed to find the net throughout the rest of the season. Hartley played a big part in an FA Cup run that saw Everton beaten by Derby County in the semi-final at Molineux. He then left Everton and signed for Liverpool.

He seemed to lose his goal scoring touch at Anfield and left the club having scored just one goal in 12 league and FA Cup games. He then played Southern League football with Southampton and helped them to win the championship. Abe then played for Woolwich Arsenal before ending his career by playing 13 league games for. Burnley. He finally settled in Southampton where he took a job with L& SW Railway Company and collapsed and died, 9 9 1909, at the company's Engine Shed on Southampton Docks. He was 37 years old.

Alexander Stewart was born, 1868, in Greenock and began his playing football for his local club Morton before signing for Burnley in 1889. He spent three seasons at Turf Moor before accepting the offer to join Everton where he made his debut, 17 12 1892, in a home match against Notts County. Alex Stewart spent a short, but eventful, time at Goodison Park. He represented Everton in 12 league games and played in all seven matches during the arduous FA Cup campaign of 1893. Alex Stewart left Everton during the summer of 1893 to join Nottingham Forest

William S Stewart was signed to replace his fellow clansman Alex, and proved to be one of the finest players ever to grace the confines of Goodison Park. He immediately settled in to the Everton half back line where his massive frame became quite the foil to the play of both Jonny Holt and Dickie Boyle. The Scot was reported to be one of the best and most graceful moving players of his generation and arrested the attention of all those who saw him play. He was tall, strong and could throw the ball from the touchline, a great distance, and was a difficult man to knock off the ball. He was, in fact, one of the best early signings the club made.

William Stephen Stewart was born, 26 3 1867, at 16 Ogalvie Street, Arbroath to textile millworker whose name was Mary. He grew in the fishing port and, after working as a baker, decided on a career with the British Army. He enlisted in the Black Watch and was later transferred to the Royal Scots Greys and was posted to their cavalry barracks in the North of Ireland. He won many honours while playing football in the army and also represented the Irish League side, Distillery. He first appeared for the Irish club, in 1888, against the Blackburn based side Witton who were on tour in Ireland. Stewart also helped the same club, 16 3 1889, to an Irish Cup victory over the YMCA. Next season he made his first appearance on Mainland Britain, 18 1 1890, when he represented the Distillery club in an FA Cup tie against Bolton Wanderers at Pikes Lane. The Irish amateurs lost the game by 10 goals to 2. Nevertheless, the skill displayed by Billy Stewart alerted the interest of Preston North End who agreed to purchase his discharge from the Army that allowed him to sign professional forms with the Deepdale club. The experience he gained in the Royal Scots

Greys enabled him to obtain employment as a groom while they found him lodgings, along with two other of their players, at 64 North Road in Preston. Billy Stewart played two seasons at Preston before accepting an invitation to join Everton in August 1893.

Quickly daubed with the moniker of "Soldier" Stewart, the Scot settled quickly in to the Everton set up and missed only one league match during his inaugural season at Goodison Park. He became a regular fixture at wing half and played a big part in Everton's victory in the first Merseyside derby game against Liverpool. The "Soldier" soon became an automatic selection at wing half and was a member of the 1897 FA Cup side who lost to Aston Villa at Crystal Palace. He took over the club captaincy in 1897 and was part of the disappointing side that lost the FA Cup semi-final against Derby County at Wolverhampton. Stewart then lost favour with the selectors and was not retained at the end of season. He had played 137 league and cup games for Everton and scored 6 goals. In 1898 the "Soldier" accepted an offer to join Southern League side Bristol City and remained there for two seasons. He made 51 league appearances for the West Country club before returning, with his wife, to Liverpool.

On 9th July 1901 Billy Stewart is on record when he registers the birth of his son Stanley who later died, the same year, along with his first wife Emma. He did, at this time, give his profession as a victualler and his address as 22 Balfour Road. In 1911 he remarried a Liverpool lady named Ellen and they lived at 1 Cameron Street and he worked as a dock labourer. He later received an injury while working on the Liverpool waterfront that was to cause him pain for the rest of his life. His last major appearance came at the Philharmonic Hall when he addressed the assembly on the occasion of the club's Jubilee Dinner. He spoke of the many changes that had come over the game and recalled times when the game was simple. The "Soldier" claimed that the modern footballers were pampered and speeded up instead of being allowed to show their natural football ability. He traced back to the days when there were no goal nets, when a penalty came from a ringed portion of the goal, when goalkeepers were taken to earth while another forward took to shooting for goal. Billy "Soldier" Stewart spent the final years of his life residing at Cedar Grove off Lodge Lane. In 1937 he took ill and was admitted to Sefton General Hospital where he died and was buried at Toxteth Park Cemetery.

Robert Kelso was one of most gifted halfbacks ever to have pulled on an Everton jersey. He arrived in Liverpool via Preston North End, having previously had a most successful career in Scotland. Kelso was born in 1865 at Cardross, Dumbartonshire and gained two Scottish cup winners medals with Renton where he won seven caps for his country. In 1887 Kelso crossed the border and spent one season as an amateur on Tyneside with Newcastle West End. On the 19 1 1888 he made a surprise appearance at Anfield where he assisted Everton, in a single league game, against Preston North End. Major Sudall, no doubt, was impressed by the performance of Kelso who accepted his offer to join him at Deepdale.

In the summer of 1891, following a successful spell at Preston, Kelso returned to Everton where he partnered John Holt and Hope Robertson in the half back line. He was an ever-present in the FA Cup run that saw Everton lose to Wolves in their first FA Cup final in Manchester. Bob Kelso is assured of a place in the record book by being the player who registered the first goal for Everton that was scored from the penalty spot. The goal was scored on the Thornyholme cricket ground, 25 2 1893, in a match against Accrington and around 300 excursionists from Liverpool were present to witness the event. Everton, it was reported, had the ball in the net but the referee, Mr. Fitzroy-Norris of Bolton, brought back the play and ordered a penalty kick to be taken. Kelso then beat Hay in the Accrington goal to give Everton a 3-0 victory. Bob Kelso spent five seasons with Everton playing in 103 league and cup games and scoring five goals. He left Everton in 1896 and returned to Scotland where he played for Dundee before ending his career, as an amateur, with Bedminster Town, He died 10 8 1942.

Jack Daniel Taylor was undoubtedly the most versatile Scotsman ever to wear an Everton shirt and one of the club's most loyal and devoted servants. He was born, 27 1 1872, at 19 Clyde Street, Dumbarton where his father worked as a shipwright on the shores of the River Clyde. He first of all played junior football before joining the Dumbarton club and helped them to twice win the Scottish championships on consecutive occasions. Taylor played his final game for Dumbarton, 17 3 1894, and then accepted an invitation to join St Mirren for whom he scored 12 goals in 27 appearances. In May 1896 he left the Paisley based club and journeyed to Liverpool where he started what was to be a long and eventful career with Everton.

Jack Taylor, playing on the right wing, was in the Everton side when they opened the season with a friendly match against Glasgow Rangers at Goodison Park. He then made his debut on the opening day of the league season and scored in a 2-1 win over Sheffield Wednesday. On 16th January he scored a hat trick against West Bromwich Albion before Everton embarked on the FA Cup run that took Everton through to their first appearance in the final. Jack Taylor was a member of the side that was beaten by Wolverhampton Wanderers in the final. He then took part in all 30 of the league games that were played next season and was not absent from the line up until March 1890 having, by then, taken part in over 120 league matches. He was selected to represent Scotland on four occasions and scored one goal. Jack Taylor was a member of the Everton side that won the FA Cup in 1907 and also took part in the unsuccessful final, against Sheffield Wednesday, one year later. The Scot went on to make over 400 appearances for an Everton team where he was equally at home among the forwards as he was in defence. He was also a regular goal scorer. His career came to an abrupt end in the 1910 FA Cup semi-final against Barnsley when the ball hit him in his windpipe. The blow damaged his larynx and this effectively put an end to his career as a professional footballer. Jack Taylor later played a few games in the Everton reserve side before ending his playing days as an amateur with South Liverpool. He is, to date, one of six players to play over 450 games for Everton and is ranked seventh in their all time appearance table. In later life he lived in Trafalgar Road, Wallasey and died, following a car crash, in 1949.

James Jamieson was born, 3 11 1867, in the lowland town of Lockerbie and joined Everton during the summer of 1892. He first featured in the club's combination side before making his first team debut on 15th October away against Newton Heath in Manchester. The two clubs had met three weeks previously, but the game had had to be abandoned due to a heavy downpour of rain. Jamieson played 14 league games in the Everton half back line but saw his chances of further games reduced by the signing of "Soldier" Stewart from Preston North End. He decided on a move across the Pennines where he made over one hundred league appearances for Sheffield Wednesday.

Alan Maxwell was signed to strengthen the Everton forward line two weeks after the club had temporarily lost the services of Fred Geary through injury. He was born, 1870, in Glasgow and came to Merseyside having previously played for Third Lanark. Maxwell made his debut in a strong reserve side that had been assembled for the visit of the re-enforced second eleven of Accrington. He made his first team debut, 31 10 1891, away at Preston where Everton were beaten by 4 goals to 0. Alan Maxwell spent three seasons with Everton scoring 13 goals in 43 league appearances. He was also an "ever-present" in the club's mammoth FA Cup campaign of 1893 scoring the vital goal that finally put paid to Preston North End in the semi-final at Blackburn. Alan Maxwell, in the face of stiff opposition, failed to secure a regular first team place and left Everton to join Darwen at their home on Barley Bank Meadow. He later signed for Stoke in a rather bizarre transfer deal that involved a pair of wrought iron gates before ending his playing days with the St Bernard club in Edinburgh.

James Adams was a fullback who began playing football with the Norton Park junior club in his native Edinburgh before signing for Hearts in 1885. He was born, 17 8 1864, and was a member of the Heart of Midlothian side who became founder members of the Scottish League. He gained his first Scottish cap, 9 3 1889, against Ireland and represented his country on another two occasions. Jimmy Adams will always be remembered as the man, who by his actions, made the need for a penalty kick to be introduced in Scottish Football when in the cup-tie against East Stirling, he prevented a goal by deliberately handling the ball on the goal line. He remained at Tynecastle for over eight seasons and played as an amateur over 100 games for his club. His marriage lines, which were written in 1889, tell us he was then living at Fountainbridge and was employed as a mason (journeyman). His wife, whose maiden name was Stirling, was Fanny Adams. In 1891 the couple were living on the Gorgie Road and it was from this location that they moved to Liverpool.

The Heart of Midlothian team circa 1895

Jimmy Adams (back row) stands third from left while Archibald McKinnon is seated third from left.

The signings of Jimmy Adams, along with Tom McInnes, considerably strengthened the defensive qualities of an Everton side that had, the previous season, finished sixth in the table. The forward players, led by Jack Southworth, were all capable of scoring goals and hopes of the fans soared when, 19 8 1894 Adams made his debut in a home win match against Sheffield Wednesday. Everton made a whirlwind start to the season and had won all seven league games when, 13 10 1894, they faced local rivals Liverpool in the first ever Merseyside derby game at Goodison Park. Jimmy Adams, who captained the home side, led Everton to a 3-0 victory. Next week disaster struck when Everton lost the services of Jack Southworth with an injury that ended his career as they went down 4-3 against Blackburn Rovers at Ewood Park. Adams who had an indifferent game lost his regular place in the team. He went on to make another twelve appearances for the club as Everton finished runners-up to Sunderland. Next season Adams fared better at Goodison missing only two league games as Everton finished third in the table. He accompanied Everton on their lengthy end-of-season tour before returning to Scotland and his old club, Heart of Midlothian. He had made 43 league and cup appearances for Everton and scored one goal.

Jimmy Adams spent one last season at Tynecastle before retiring from the game and became a referee. He later emigrated to America where he resumed his trade as a stonemason before dying, 24 4 1943 in New Jersey.

Thomas McInnes is assured of a special place in Everton folklore by being the first player to score a goal in a Merseyside derby game. He was born 22 3 1877 in Glasgow where he first played football with Cowlairs before joining Notts County in 1889. He remained with the east Midlands club for 3 seasons before returning to his native city where he signed for Third Lanark. Tom McInnes was a member of the Third Lanark team who, 19 4 1894, took to the field to oppose Everton at in match, played at Goodison Park, which was watched by 6,000 people. The event had been arranged for the benefit of former Everton player Danny Kirkwood who had recently broken his leg while playing for Liverpool Caledonians.

Whether or not the Everton board approached McInnes that evening is not clear but what was certain is that he made his debut for the club, 1 9 1894, in the opening match of the next season and scored in a 3-1 win at the expense of Sheffield Wednesday. Everton then won their next six league matches before, 13-4-1894 they faced Liverpool in the first ever Merseyside derby game at Goodison Park.

The match produced scenes not previously seen in Liverpool as around 40,000 poured through the turnstiles at Goodison Park producing record gate receipts of £1,026. Jimmy Adams led out the home side alongside the former Everton fullback Andrew Hannah who was now captain of Liverpool. Everton made a bright start to the game and Tom McInnes gave them the lead after 10 minutes. The same player then left the field with an injury but was back in action when Alex Latta doubled the lead for his side on the hour. Liverpool then fought hard to retrieve the game but a late third goal scored by Jack Bell finally broke their resistance. McInnes played a big part in the championship challenge made by Everton who, eventually, finished runners-up to Sunderland. He spent one more season at Goodison and left having scored 18 goals in 47 league and cup games.

Tom McInnes left Everton to join Luton Town who had first made a successful application to join the Football League accepted. The Bedfordshire club however found the venture too expensive and rejoined the United League after just one season. McInnes played for the club for three seasons before ending his playing days with the Queens Engineering Works in Bedford. Tom McInnes died in Luton, in 1959.

John Collins was essentially a player who was signed to re-enforce the position of full back and always could relied upon when asked to deputize for an injured player. He joined Everton during the summer of 1892 from the Scottish Division one side Cambuslang and made his debut, 17 9 1892; in a 5-2 home win over Darwen. He then appeared in the two league games that followed. However he failed to command a regular first team place and left Everton in the spring of 1893. John Collins had played 15 league games for Everton.

Archibald Pinnell was one of several players signed by Everton during the 1891-92 season and is typical of the many Scotsmen who decided to try their luck in England. He was born, 1870, in the Ayrshire town of Stevenson from where, with his family, he moved to the coal-mining town of Blanytre in north Lanarkshire. In 1891 Archie is reported to be living, with his parents and three brothers, at 7 Bairds Row in the Stonefield area of the town and is working, along with his father and elder brother, as a miner in the local colliery owned by William Baird. His versatile football talents were first noticed while he was playing with Blantyre Victoria and it was from this football club that he joined Everton in September 1891.

He made his debut on October 25th, in a specially arranged reserve team fixture against Accrington that was played at Anfield. Both sides, it had been agreed, would field a strong side. Pinnell, who played at centre forward, helped Everton to win the game by 2 goals to 0. He then played out the season, in various positions, in the club's combination side. Archie Pinnell made his first team debut, 17 9 1892, against Blackburn Rovers at Ewood Park where he took up the position of goalkeeper. Everton were leading 2-0 when a late fight back earned the home side a 2-2 draw .A local journalist had this to say about his performance... *Pinnell kept goal surprisingly well, endearing many ugly shots, and on each occasion he was beaten he had played the ball first, only to see it scrimmaged through. He did not chuck or punch the sphere with sufficient power when the fatal attacks were made. He merely returned the ball to the scrimmages a fault he would overcome by experience in either putting the ball over the bar or throwing it aside. Pinnell made a good impression as an emergency custodian, and should improve by coaching from the experience colleagues. (Liverpool Mercury 19 9 1892.)* Pinnell, who retained his place, made home debut next Saturday and was a virtual spectator as Everton demolished the newly promoted Newton Heath by 6 goals to 0. His third and final first team game came two weeks later against the current league champions, Sunderland. The Wearsiders, dubbed "The team of all Talents", proved too good for the home side and beat them by 4 goals to 1. Archie Pinnell returned to the Everton combination side where he remained until the end of the season. He then joined Preston North End.

Archie spent one season at Deepdale and was selected to play for the first eleven on only one occasion. He spent most of the time playing reserve football before deciding to join nearby Chorley who played their football in the Lancashire League. Archie soon became the regular goalkeeper with the Lancashire club and helped to win the league championship in 1896. He remained at Chorley for four years before being persuaded to join Burnley. Archie spent one season with the Turf Moor club and took part in 5 league games before deciding to join New Brompton where he played football in the Southern League. He then enlisted in the army. Archie joined the Scots Guards where his army papers reveal that his next of kin was listed as his brother William. It is likely that he fought in Boer War and returned to England from South Africa for in 1903 he suddenly re-appears in the colours of Plymouth Argyle having joined them from a local amateur side named Oreston Rovers. He represented Plymouth Argyle on seven occasions during their first season in the Southern League and then returned to play for Oreston Rovers.

He later returned to Blantyre and took up his old job as a coal miner. On 15th July 1915 Archie, now 39 years old and still a Bachelor, married a widow named Agnus Reynolds at 35 Hutchenson Street in Glasgow. The marriage certificate reveals that Agnus is a hospital nurse and she has a home in Blantyre. Archie Pinnell then re-joined the Scots Guards for, as his army records shows, he was placed in charge of Chinese Labour Corp in France. The date is September 1915. He survived the conflict and returned to Scotland where he again took up employment as a coal miner. Archie Pinnell, having survived his wife, was 78 when he died at Hamilton on the day before a newly promoted Everton side beat Chelsea 2-0 before a crowd of 60,000 at Stamford Bridge. The date was September 1954.

Samuel Thompson, along with Nick Ross, was part of the all-conquering Preston North End team of the late 1880s and was near the end of his career when he came to Everton from Wolverhampton Wanderers. He was born, 1862, in the Ayrshire coalfield where, while playing for Lugar Boswell, his skilful forward play first caught the eye of the Scottish selectors. Thompson made his International debut, 29 3 1884, against Wales at Cathkin Park, Glasgow and gained his second cap against Ireland at Belfast, three weeks later. Next season he played a couple of friendly matches with Glasgow Rangers from where he was persuaded, by Major Sudall, to join the formidable side he was constructing at Preston. Thompson played a major role in the Preston double winning side and scored one of the goals, against Wolves, in the 1889 FA Cup final. However, following this most successful period of his career, he secretly agreed to sign for Wolverhampton Wanderers who picked up a £50 fine for having approached the player illegally. Sam Thompson left Wolverhampton during the summer of 1891 and made his debut for Everton in the opening league match of the new football season.

Everton were the current league champions when they took to field against West Bromwich Albion on their home ground at Stoney Lane. Thompson, who took the place of Pat Gordon, played at inside forward as Everton, who gave a disjointed display, were surprisingly beaten by 4 goals to 0. His appearance however, caused something of a surprise and it caused one local reporter to publish the following comments…*Sam Thompson, who played for Wolverhampton last season, looks like being a very dear bargain for Everton. He asked for £3.5s a week, and was eventually engaged at £3, a long price for such an ancient player (Liverpool Mercury.)* Thompson, nevertheless, retained his place and made his home debut against Darwen four days later. Everton, who played much better won the game by 5 goals to 3. He then scored in his third and final game for Everton, at home to Preston North End before leaving the club to join Accrington where he spent the remaining time of his career. Sam Thompson later managed a public house in Preston where he died on 23rd December 1943.

Richard Boyle was a halfback who served Everton faithfully for over ten seasons. He was born, 24 9 1869, in Dumbarton and was a member of the local side that, in 1892, won the Scottish League championship. Following this success Boyle left Scotland and signed for Everton and was a member of the side who played in the inaugural match against Nottingham Forest at Goodison Park. He quickly adapted to life in England playing another 23 games during his first season in the football league. Dickie Boyle was also an ever-present in the Everton side that first reached the FA Cup final where he was involved in the now famous incident which led the winning goal being scored against Everton by the Wolves captain Harry Allen.

The English press, in the days leading up to the game, had made much of the seven Scottish players present in the Everton team while their opponents were made up entirely of Englishmen. The Midland fans, as they arrived on the ground, displayed cards in the bands of the hat on which was printed the words "Play up England" Around 30,000 people were expected to attend the game but double that amount were reported to have paid for admission. The pressure of crowd caused the barriers to collapse and the spectators got so close to the touchline that they frequently interfered with play. Dickie Boyle, when attempting to control the ball, appeared to have it kicked from his possession by a member of the crowd. The incident led, indirectly to Allen scoring the only goal of the game. The Everton executive, angry at the incident, made their feelings known to the authorities but, after due consideration, decided not to enter a formal protest. Boyle was also one of the seven Scotsmen that was part of the Everton side who contested the 1901 FA Cup final and scored one of the goals as they were beaten 3-2 by Aston Villa. He was also an ever-present during two football league seasons and took part in the first ever Merseyside derby game. Richard Boyle played, what was then, a record 243 league and cup games and scored eight goals before leaving Everton to join Dundee in 1902. **John Bell** was the final member of the formidable trio of players who joined Everton from the Dumbarton area, during the early

1890s. He was born, 6 10 1869, in Dumbarton and began his football career with the local club. Bell was a player who regularly scored goals from his favourite position on the right wing and he represented the Sons of the Rock during their first two seasons in the Scottish League. He topped the goal scoring table on both occasions. Dumbarton, in the inaugural season, had tied for the title with Rangers and SFA ordered the two sides to stage a championship play-off match at Cathkin Park in Glasgow. John Bell, along with Richard Boyle, took part in the match that ended in a draw so the championship was declared a tie. In 1890 Bell won the first of his ten International caps for Scotland. In March 1892 he left Dumbarton for what was to be the first of his two spells with Everton.

Bell made his debut, 3 4 1892, against Bolton Wanderers at Goodison Park and played in the other two league games that were required to complete the fixture list that season. The goal scoring exploits of Jack Southworth was the main feature of the season that followed yet the Everton team, who scored ninety goals, finished a disappointing sixth in the table. Jack Bell, following an injury to Southworth, became the club's leading goal scorer with 18 goals, one of which came in the first derby game against Liverpool at Goodison Park. Jack Bell was, in 1896, the first Everton player to score a goal in an FA Cup final. He was an active AFU member and this may have caused him to move from Goodison and spend a brief spell with Tottenham Hotspur before being persuaded to return to Scotland at the invitation of Celtic.

The experienced Bell then won two Scottish cup winners medals with Celtic and scored their first goal of the 20TH century. He scored 23 goals for the Glasgow club before returning to Liverpool where he opened a bicycle shop and played football with New Brighton Tower. One year later Bell returned to Everton and scored twice in the opening match of the 1901-02 season against Manchester City at Goodison Park. It was to be another heartbreaking season for the Goodison faithful who saw their team pipped for the title by a Sunderland side who they had done the double over in the league. At the end of next season Jack Bell left Everton for a coaching job with Preston North End having played 199 games and scored 70 goals.

David Storrier was a powerfully built defender who was born, 17 11 1872, and began his football career with a junior team who played under the name of Dauntless before, in 1892, joining his hometown club of Arbroath. His talents did not go unnoticed and

soon a local scout was on his doorstep to offer him a professional contract with Everton, which he accepted.

Storrier was first chosen to represent the Everton senior eleven in a friendly match against Dundee at West Craigie Park and then became a regular member of the club's Combination side. The Scot made an unpretentious start to his Everton career playing just five league and cup games during his first two campaigns. However, he then established himself in time to be selected for the 1897 FA Cup final where he teamed up with Peter Meechan at full back. He was an active member of the Association Footballers Union that was more or less led by the Scottish players at Everton. Peter Storrier played 55 league and cup games for Everton before he left to join Celtic in May 1898.

Dave Storrier as depicted in the 1897 FA Cup final.

The Glasgow club offered Storrier the captaincy and he led them to a Scottish Cup triumph in 1899. The same year he was selected to play for Scotland in all three home internationals and captained them on one occasion. (He also captained his country at cricket.) He went on to play 40 games for Celtic before leaving in 1901 to play ten games for Dundee. His career however, was to have a sting in the tail.

The itinerant Scot again moved south at the invitation of Millwall Athletic where his pathway through life again brought him in to contact with Everton. On 7th March 1903, Dave Storrier lined up to face the "Toffees" in a 3rd round FA Cup tie, played at East Ferry Road, to decide which club would go through to the semi-final. The

Londoners won the tie, with a single goal that was scored after 25 minutes. Storrier played a prominent roll by keeping a close watch on Jack Sharp but missed a penalty late in the game. David Storrier, his playing days at an end, returned to live in Arbroath were he died, 27 1 1910, at the young age of 37.

Robert Gary was a speedy left sided player who was signed to cover the club's weakness in that department. He was born 1878, in Glasgow and began playing junior football with Lenzie FC before making his Scottish League debut, 17 4 1897, in a division two match for Partick Thistle against Kilmarnock. The Jags went on to gain promotion. Gray then remained a further two seasons with the Jags before joining Everton in time to enjoy the club's pre-season sports day that took place that year, at the Stanley Hotel in Aughton.

Robert Gray's first taste of English football came with the club's reserve side at such unfashionable places as Astley Bridge and Skerton before scoring on his first team debut, 23 12 1899, in a 2-1 win over Manchester City at Hyde Road. This was unfortunately the only goal that Robert Gray would score for Everton in the two seasons he spent at Goodison Park. He failed to gain a regular place in the first eleven playing just 21 league and cup games before departing to try his luck on the south coast with Southampton.

Robert Gray stayed one season with the Southern League outfit before returning home to re-join Partick Thistle at Meadowside. He quickly gained himself a regular place in the side and took part in over 160 league and cup matches. His playing days over, Gray moved to the town of Kirkintilloch. He became a member of the committee at the local Rob Roy FC and lived out the rest of his days in the east Dumbartonshire town. In June 1959, Robert Gray spent the last day of his life on a pensioners' outing to the seaside town of Largs but died at his home shortly after his return. He was 83.

Hugh Goldie was born, 10 2 1874, in the Ayrshire town of Dalry where he played junior football for the nearby Hurlford club before being asked to join St Mirren club at their home in Paisley. It was while playing with the Buddies that Goldie was invited to have a trial for Everton while the club was on tour in Scotland. He impressed the club directorate and accepted their invitation to come to Liverpool in the summer of 1895. He played in the pre-season trial game and took part in the club's annual sports day at the Grapes Hotel in Freshfield before making his first team debut, 9 9 1895, in a home game against Bury. Goldie was to play in 20 league and FA Cup games for Everton and score one goal. He then lost his place but regained it following an injury to Holt in the home match, 19 10 1895, against West Bromwich Albion. He held his place in a 14 match unbeaten run until being dropped following a disastrous 4-0 FA Cup defeat by Sheffield Wednesday at the Olive Grove. Goldie then played just one more league game, a defeat at Derby County, as Everton finished third in the table. The Scot returned to the club next season but failed to find a regular place in a very competitive Everton half back line. He took part in the opening match at Goodison Park, a friendly with Glasgow Rangers, but was not selected again for the first eleven until, 31 9 1896, when he took part in a goalless draw with Wolves. He played just two more league games for Everton before returning to Scotland at the invitation of the Celtic club in Glasgow.

Hugh Goldie played 27 games for the Parkhead club before being forced, by their strict financial measures, to leave and join Dundee in January 1899. Goldie later found himself playing football in South Wales with Barry Town before moving to spend one season with Millwall Athletic during the summer of 1889. Hugh Goldie played at the heart of the Southern League sides defence during historical FA Cup campaign which included a sensational win over Aston Villa before going down to Southampton in the semi-final. The itinerant Scotsmen then moved back north to play for Dundee before returning south to end his playing career with Southern

The 1898 squad
Back row: D Friel (Trainer), R Davidson, Alex King, W Maley (Manager), Willie Orr, John Hodge, Tom Hynds
Middle row (seated): D Storrier, B Battles, H Goldie, J Welford, D Doyle, J Campbell, A McMahon, P Gilhooly
Front row: J Fisher, Dan McArthur, Jack Bell

Hugh Goldie seen in the Celtic team along with Jack Bell, Danny Doyle and Dave Storrier. Manager W Maley also played for Everton.

League side, New Brompton. Hugh Goldie, his playing days at an end, returned to his native Ayrshire where he ran a public house at Hurlford.

John Cameron was to have a varied and interesting a life as any player who ever wore the colours of Everton Football Club. He was born, 13 4 1872 in the west coast seaside town of Ayr and began playing football with Ayr Parkhouse FC. Cameron, around 1893, later moved to Clydeside where, while working at the local office of the Cunard Shipping Line, he accepted the invitation to play football with the famous Queens Park amateur club in Glasgow. It was during this time that Cameron won his only international cap when he took part 3-3, against Ireland, on the Solitude ground in Belfast. In September 1895, he signed a contract with Everton that was to place him amongst the highest paid football players in the football league.

John Cameron made his Everton debut, 5 10 1895; in a 5-0 home win over Sheffield United. There are conflicting reports concerning his part in the game. The official club records omit him from the score sheet while the *Liverpool Mercury*, 7 10 1895, credits him with scoring the second goal. He did nevertheless play 16 league and FA Cup matches before the end of the season and is credited with scoring on 5 occasions. Cameron got the 1896-97 league campaign off to a good start by scoring the first goal of the season against Sheffield Wednesday. He then scored a hat trick, at home to Burnley, but managed just one more goal at home to Stoke between then and the end of season. Cameron then became involved, along with Jack Bell, in the formation of the footballers' union.

The Football League clubs, or more precisely their directors, were attempting to impose a wage restriction of £4 per week on all players' wages and the likes of John Cameron, who was proberbly on double that amount, saw this as a threat to their livelihood. Furthermore, the clubs had recently implemented a registration scheme that bound the player to them and forbade him from any negotiations concerning his transfer. In February 1898 the Association Footballers Union was announced with John Cameron acting as secretary. Jack Bell was named as the organization's first president. The two Scots, in the meantime, continued to turn out for Everton.

The season 1897-98 was to be the last John Cameron was to spend with Everton playing 22 league matches and scoring just three goals. His last appearance came, 22 2 1898, against Sheffield United. He also took part in two FA Cup ties scoring his last goal for the club in a replay against Stoke. John Cameron, it would appear, lost favour with the Everton selectors and never played for the first eleven again. His last major appearance in an Everton shirt was in the Liverpool Senior Cup final against New Brighton Tower. He left Everton during the summer and took the player/managers role at Tottenham Hotspur.

John Cameron was to prove a great servant to the north London club leading them to FA Cup glory by being the first team, from outside the Football League, to lift the trophy in 1901. In 1907 he left London to take up a coaching job with German club, Dresden and was interned, during World War One, at the notorious Ruhleben Sportsmen's Camp along with Sam Wolstenholme who had also played for Everton. Cameron, when the armistice was declared, returned to the west coast of Scotland where he became the manager of his hometown club, Ayr United. He later became a full time journalist before he died, 20 4 1935, in Glasgow.

John Tait Robertson was a central defender who joined Everton, along with John Cameron, from the Queens Park club in Glasgow. He was born, 25 2 1887, at Dumbarton where he played junior football with Sinclair Swifts before joining the famous amateur club on their home ground at Hampden Park. Robertson first accepted the invitation to play one league game for Everton, as an amateur, before returning to Scotland. He agreed to sign professional forms after playing one more game for Everton, 23 4 1896, against Celtic in Glasgow.

Jacky Robertson played reserve team football with Everton until, 6 4 1896, when he made his first team debut in a 1-1 home draw with Bolton Wanderers. Next season his record improved slightly when he appeared in four league and cup games. Robertson finally established himself as a regular member of the first team halfback line following injury to Alex Stewart in a bad tempered game away at Derby. He then played in 26 league games and was ever-present in the FA Cup campaign that ended so disastrously in the semi-final against Derby County at Molineux. He scored his only goal for Everton, on Christmas Day, against Aston Villa at Goodison Park and made his last appearance, 23 4 1898, in a friendly against Queens Park Rangers in London. Robertson then quietly departed for the south coast.

Southampton was his destination where he helped the Hampshire club to win the Southern League in 1899. He spent one season on the south coast before returning to Scotland where he signed for Glasgow Rangers. Jacky Robertson spent the most successful part of his career at Ibrox Park where he eventually became the club captain. He won 16 Scottish Caps and helped Rangers to win the league championship on three consecutive occasions. He played 130 league and cup games with the Ibrox club before accepting the role of player/manager with Chelsea. Who had recently been elected to the football league. Indeed it was Robertson who scoreed the first goal, away ay blackpool, for the Standford Bridge Club in their new venture he later became player/manager of Glossop before ending his career as reserve team coach with Manchester United. John T Robertson was 57 when he died, 1 9 1935, at Milton in Wiltshire.

William Henderson was an 18-year-old full back who joined Everton from Broxburn Athletic in November 1896. Unable to break in to the senior eleven he moved to Reading at the end of season and remained there for four seasons. In the summer of 1901 he moved to Southampton. Henderson had to battle for the full back spot with the famous amateur C.B. Fry and was always obliged to stand down whenever the polymath was available for selection. Left out of the 1902 Southampton FA Cup final side, Henderson headed back to Goodison Park and re-signed for Everton.

The full back had never completely severed his links with Everton because he had, during his time in the south, made a couple of guest appearances for the club. In September 1902, Henderson at last got his wish when he pulled on the club jersey for the first time but could not prevent Everton from encountering a defeat at the hands of Newcastle United. Unable to command a regular place in an indifferent Everton side, Henderson made his final league appearance in a controversial home match with Blackburn Rovers before returning to Elm Park to play for Reading. He later played for Clapton Orient before ending his career with the Southern League side, New Brompton.

John Patrick was a goalkeeper who was born, 10 1 1870, at Kilsyth and played football with Grangemouth and Falkirk before settling down with the St Mirren club in Paisley. On 28 10 1896, he played one football league game for Everton and assisted them to a 6-0 win over Burnley. His sudden appearance in Liverpool is something of a mystery, as the local newspapers give no hint of his expected arrival. What is certain is that John Patrick does all that is required of him and his performance was much appreciated by the crowd at Goodison Park. He then returned to Scotland where he continued his career with St Mirren.

However, the Everton executive must have noticed some degree of quality in the play of John Patrick because, 20 3 1897, he won his first Scottish cap when he kept goal for his country against Wales at Wrexham. He then won the second of his two caps when, 3 4 1897, he kept goal for Scotland in a 2-1 win over England at the Crystal Palace. John Patrick was to prove a faithful servant to St Mirren and kept goal for them on 149 occasions.

Peter Meechan was a strong willed individual whose football career was to be as colourful as it was controversial. He was born, 28 2 1872, at Uphall, West Lothian the son of an Irish born miner who had found work in the local shale pits. Meechan started his working life as a shale miner and played football amongst the local clubs before joining Hibernian from Broxburn FC in 1892. Meechan was a class footballer whose skill and determination soon caught the eye of Sunderland for whom, after agreeing to their terms, he turned professional in 1893 and moved to England. He was to have a successful spell with the Wearside club playing over 50 league and cup games and helping them to win the championship in 1894. Meechan was then upset by the remarks made by a Scottish politician which appeared in a West Lothian newspaper that appeared to object to him living south of the Tweed while still remaining on the voting register in Scotland. In May 1895 he returned to Scotland and signed for Celtic. Sunderland, however, still held his contract. Meechan soon settled back his homeland helping Celtic to win the championship in 1896. Things appeared to be going well for him and he won his only Scottish cap, against Ireland, during his time with Celtic. However, he was soon forced to leave Glasgow in rather controversial circumstances. Meechan, along with two other Celtic players, were offended by the remarks made by a certain journalist who criticized their performance in a local cup match with Rangers. The following home game was against Hibernian. Meechan, along with two other players, refused to take to the field until the offending journalist was removed from the press box. The request was denied so the players refused to take to the field. They later appeared before the club committee and were told that they would never be allowed to play football for Celtic again. Peter Meechan then accepted an offer to play professional football with Everton, at Goodison Park.

Everton paid a record £450 for the signature of Peter Meechan £200 of which was claimed by Sunderland who still held his contract. His arrival in Liverpool passed unnoticed and he slipped quietly in to the Everton reserve where, 31 1 1887, he played alongside John Cameron against the Bolton Wanderers second eleven at Burnden Park. Meechan made his first team debut on 2nd February in an FA Cup tie at home to Bury and aided his new club to reach the last eight of the competition with a 3-0 victory. The quality of Meechan soon caught the eye of the local press who lavished praise upon a style of play not previously seen at Goodison Park. *Great interest was taken in the play of Meechan, the latest Scottish recruit. The game had not been sometime in progress before an opportunity was afforded him of showing his ability and that he was a success on the days play was freely admitted. His style of play is vastly different from that of the general run of league backs. He tackled his men with a cool confident that must be confessed kept the Everton enthusiasts on tenterhooks as to the result, but he invariably came out right in the end, and coolly passed the ball to a half back with the air of an accomplished forward. Rash kicking was not resotored to and providing the confidant business is not overdone, he should prove invaluable in the clubs remaining fixtures. (Liverpool Mercury 15 2 1897.)* Meechan represented Everton in seven league games and helped them win the Lancashire trophy with a 2-0 win over Manchester City. He also helped them to reach the FA Cup final, played at Crystal Palace, but could not prevent an excellent Aston Villa side from completing a league and cup double. The Scot was to spend a trouble free eighteen months with Everton playing in all 28 league and cup games but was never fortunate enough to find the back of the net. He eventually appeared to lose favour with the selectors and played his last senior game, 15 1 1898, in a 1-1 home draw with Stoke. Peter Meecham, however, appeared to have played out the rest of the season without ceremony for, on 22nd

April, he is amongst an Everton XI that had been selected to take part in a football match that was designed to draw public attention to the new home of Queens Park Rangers at Kensal Rise in west London. At the end of season, he left Everton to join Southampton.

It was most likely the offer of higher wages that took Meechan to the south coast for he was now married with a family. Nevertheless, he helped Southampton to win the Southern League championship on three occasions before falling in to conflict with club management over an issue of team selection. Meecham next had a short spell with Manchester City before moving on to play non-league football with Barrow and thereafter ending his playing days back home with Broxburn Athletic. The Meechan family, in 1905, emigrated to Canada in the hope of securing a better way of life. Meechan tried to find work in the football industry of North America but eventually was forced back to working as a miner. He died, June 1915, at his home in St Morien, Nova Scotia leaving a wife and seven children.

John Divers was an accomplice of Peter Meechan who had also refused to take the field at Celtic Park in the row over the presence of a certain journalist in the press box. He was born, 19 1 1874, in the Calton area of Glasgow and began playing junior football with the Vale of Clyde from where he first came to prominence while playing for the Hibernian club in Edinburgh. In September 1893 Divers joined Celtic and helped them to win two league championships before falling in to conflict with his employers at Parkhead. He left Glasgow for Liverpool in May 1897.

The former Celt was a skilful right-sided player who was signed as a replacement for Alf Millward who had recently left Everton to play football with New Brighton Tower. He made his Everton debut, 11 9 1897, and scored their only goal in a 5-1 defeat at the hands of Derby County at the Baseball Ground. Divers quickly formed a firm partnership with Edgar Chadwick that was broken only when he was injured in the Lancashire Cup tie with Bolton Wanderers early in the New Year. He later returned and played in every position in the forward line from where he had scored, when the season ended, eleven league goals. John Divers returned from Glasgow at the end of summer but struggled to establish himself in an Everton forward line that was now beginning to have a distinctly English look about it. He remained in Liverpool until 15 10 1898, when, with his previous misdemeanors behind him, he returned to Glasgow and re-signed for Celtic. The Scot left a good record behind him at Goodison having scored 11 goals in 32 games.

John Divers was part of the Celtic team that won the Scottish cup in 1898. He later went on loan to Hibernian and was a member of the team who won the Scottish cup, by beating Celtic in the 1902 final. He retired from the game in 1904 and took on the trainer's job at the Bohemians club in Dublin. John Divers, who later worked as a general labourer, died at Glasgow in 1942.

John Watson first played junior football in Dundee where he was born in 1871. In 1894/95 he played football for Dundee Wanderers assisting the club through the one season they spent in the Division Two of the Scottish League. The home of the Wanderers club, Clepington Park, later changed its name to Tannadice Park. John Watson, meanwhile, left Tayside in 1896 and spent the next two years playing his football in the Southern League with New Brompton before returning home to join the ranks of Dundee in the spring of 1898. He had played 6 games with club when 3 3 1900 Everton arrived to play a game with Dundee at Dens Park. Two weeks later, John Watson arrived in Liverpool.

He made his Everton debut, 7 1 1900 away at Derby County and played another two games before the end of the season. Watson proved to be a reliable left back who played the game in a typically Scottish fashion He spent a further 2 seasons with Everton and appeared in 44 league matches. At the end of the season Everton, along with Celtic, Rangers and Sunderland competed for the Glasgow Exhibition Cup with the gate receipts going to help the victims of the Ibrox disaster, which had occurred on 5th April 1902. Watson played his last game for Everton during the contest, and then left the club to join Tottenham Hotspur. He proved an excellent purchase for the London club and represented them in both the Southern League and FA Cup before retiring from the game in 1908.

Stanley Lawrence Bell was born in the small Clydeside town of Langmark and began his playing days on the opposite bank of the river, with Dumbarton. He later played football with Third Lanark before moving to England at the invitation of first division side, Sheffield Wednesday. Laurie Bell spent one season with the south Yorkshire side before crossing the Pennines to join Everton in the summer of 1897.

Laurie Bell made his Everton debut, 4 9 1897, and scored both goals in a 2-1 home win over Bolton Wanderers. During his first season at Everton he played alongside his namesake Jack Bell and was the club's leading scorer with fifteen league and cup goals. The season 1898-99 was to be his last with Everton. Laurie Bell gradually lost his scoring touch hitting the net for the last time, 19 11 1898, in a home match with Wolves. He spent most of the last half of the season in the reserve side making his last first team appearance, 8 4 1898 in an away game at Stoke. Bell, at the end of the season, was retained by Everton but decided his ambitions would be better served with Bolton Wanderers.

The Burnden Park club paid an undisclosed fee for his services that were reported to be substantial. Laurie Bell served the mill town club well scoring 45 goals in 103 games before being transferred to West Bromwich Albion. Bell scored 6 goals in 16 games for the "Baggies" before returning to Scotland to end his career in Edinburgh with Hibernian. Laurie Bell died in 1933.

Robert MacFarlane was a goalkeeper who was signed by the Everton directorate as a replacement for Bob Menham who had recently decided to transfer his services to Wigan County. He was born, 27 7 1876, at Greenock and played junior football with the Roseberry club before signing for Third Lanark in May 1896. He stayed with the south Glasgow club for one season before accepting the terms offered to him by Everton. Next year Rab MacFarlane made his Everton debut, 4 9 1897, against Bolton Wanderers in the opening match of the season at Goodison Park. He kept goal for Everton in the next six consecutive league games but, after some eccentric performances, he lost his place to Billy Muir. MacFarlane continued to play in the Everton reserve side until the end of season when he returned to Scotland and spent some time playing for East Stirling.

Rab MacFarlane later moved back to England where he played for Bristol St George, New Brompton and Grimsby Town before joining Celtic in May 1906. However, his eccentric behaviour appeared to persist while at Parkhead causing a local journalist, who observed his behaviour, to comment, *"when the ball is in midfield, he talks to himself, nods, gesticulates as though he were addressing a public meeting".* He later joined Middlesbrough before moving to Aberdeen where he remained until 1909. Rab MacFarlane ended his playing days with Motherwell before retiring to run his own confectionery business in his hometown of Greenock.

William Muir was yet another football player born in the Ayrshire coalfield and, for five years, he was to provide Everton with excellent service as a goalkeeper. He was born 22 9 1877 in the mining village of Muirkirk and learnt to play football at nearby Glenbuck. Known affectionately as "Gooley" he later played football with both Third Lanark and Kilmarnock before joining Everton in the summer of 1897 and made his debut, 30 10 1897, against Sheffield United.

Muir kept goal, with diligence, for Everton during a rather mundane period in the clubs history when they never appeared to be in a position to challenge for the league championship. He completed 137 league and cup games before eventually losing his place to George Kitchen who had joined Everton from Stockport County. Billy Muir was not offered another engagement in the spring of 1902 but objected to the £250 fee the club wanted for his transfer. The fee, following an appeal, was reduced to £100 and this was the price that was paid by Dundee to secure his services.

"Gooley" appeared to enjoy a long and successful period with the Tayside club because, 16 3 1907, he was selected to keep goal for Scotland in a home international match against Ireland at Celtic Park, Glasgow. It was his one and only cap. He later left Dundee to play for Bradford before ending his career with Heart-of-Midlothian in Edinburgh.

John Proudfoot was one of four brothers who began their playing career with Partick Thistle. He scored on his debut for the Glasgow club, 11 8 1894 in a game against Dundee Wanderers. Proudfoot was born, 27 4 1874, to a railway worker's family at Golden Square on the outskirts of Airdrie. There is no report of Proudfoot playing junior football locally. The family appeared to move to Glasgow where John Proudfoot served an engineering apprenticeship while playing football with Partick Thistle. In February 1897 Proudfoot joined Blackburn Rovers and scored on his debut against Bury. He played 29 games, and scored 9 goals for the Ewood Park club, before signing for Everton in May 1898.

The former Partick Thistle man was bought by Everton to play alongside Laurie Bell as John Cameron, during the summer, had left to play for Tottenham Hotspur. John Proudfoot made his debut, 1 9 1898, and scored in a 2-1 home win over Sheffield Wednesday and went on, during his first season, to hit 12 of the 48 goals scored by Everton. He played during an unspectacular period in the club's history but always managed to score his fair share of goals. His chances of first team football diminished with the signing of Sandy Young and he soon left the club. John Proudfoot scored 31 goals in 89 league and cup games during his time with Everton before moving to join the Southern League club, Watford.

The Scot, during his initial season, was suspended for insubordination and quickly left the West Hertfordshire club to return to Partick Thistle. He later took a job in the Clyde shipyards and retired from the game after spending his last season with Hamilton Academicals. John Proudfoot settled in the Whiteinch area of Glasgow where, in 1934, he died and was buried in Lambhill cemetery

Robert Beveridge was a Scottish inside forward that was signed by Everton from Nottingham Forest. He was born, 30 11 1872, in Glasgow and was playing football with Third Lanark when he accepted an invitation to join Nottingham Forest. Robert Beveridge spent one season with the east Midland club before joining Everton. He made his Everton debut, 27 10 1900, against his former employer, Nottingham Forest. Beveridge played the next three league games for Everton and then was never seen at Goodison Park again. It is not abundantly clear why Robert Beveridge suddenly left but it is likely that ill health forced him to return to his native Glasgow. He returned to his trade, a packing box maker, and took up residence, with his wife, at 13 Hallside Street in Hutchesontown district of the town. Robert Beveridge died, 11 10 1900, the cause of death being given as Phthises Pulmonadis (Consumption of the Lungs.) He was 24 years old.

John Bone was a member of a family of football players who hailed from the famous football nursery at Glenbuck in Ayrshire. There does not appear to be any record of his early playing days but he was first noticed by soccer scouts while playing for Haywood Wanderers who, in 1900, were champions of the Lanarkshire

Junior Alliance. John Bone joined Everton in the summer of 1901 and played just two first team games before leaving at the end of the season. His destination was not recorded in the Liverpool newspapers.

David Bruce Murray joined Everton in the summer of 1903 having previously played his football with Glasgow Rangers. He was born, 4 12 1883 in the Renfrewshire village of Busby where he grew, along with his brother and sisters, in the care of his two aunts who ran the local post office. He began playing junior football with Leven Victoria before joining the Ibrox club from where he made his way to Everton. Murray immediately took his place in the reserve side but was soon selected to represent the first team in their away fixture at Sheffield Wednesday. A local journalist, who accompanied the team, had this to say about his performance… *Murray, who filled in for Crelly, acquitted himself well, especially when one takes into consideration the harassing tactics adopted by the Sheffield wingers (Liverpool Courier 9 11 1903.)* Next Saturday he played his second and final league match when he took part in a bad tempered match against Sunderland at Goodison Park before playing out the rest of season with the reserve side. David Murray, who was not retained by Everton, joined Liverpool at the beginning of next season.

He spent one season at Anfield before crossing the Pennies to sign for Hull City. He later played for both Leeds City and Mexborough Town and also turned out, as an amateur, with Burslam Port Vale. In 1911, now 27, David Murray is working as a coal miner while boarding with the Sleight family at 1 Alfred Place, Mexborough and it was from there that he returned to his home village of Busby where he enlisted, 3 9 1914, in the Argyle and Sutherland Highlanders whose headquarters where at Perth. On the 9 7 1915, S/3845 Private John Murray embarked for France naming his father, James Murray of Shelston, Thurso, as being his next of kin. On 10th December 1915, David Bruce Murray of the 11the battalion Argyle and Sutherland Highlanders, was killed during the Battle of Loos and was buried in France. His last effects, £19 3s and his war medals, were awarded, after probate, to Mrs. Elizabeth Sleight of Mexborough.

Thomas McDermott was born in the Bridgeton area of Glasgow and first played football for a former nursery club of Celtic whose name was Cambuslang Hibernian. He then spent a short period on loan with Dundee before returning to make his debut for Celtic, 2 10 1901 in a 2-2 draw with Heart of Midlothian. The individual skill of McDermott quickly endeared him to home fans as he scored 4 goals in 21 league games he played for Celtic. It then came as a surprise when he suddenly left the Glasgow club because, it was reported, he had failed to comply with the pattern of training that was expected of him at Parkhead.

Tam McDermott pulled down the scale to 11 stone and was 23 years old when he joined Everton during the summer of 1903. He quickly made an impact by scoring 4 goals in the club's internal pre-season practice game. McDermott was then thrust straight into the first eleven for the opening match of 1903-04 Football League campaign against Blackburn Rovers. The visitors surprised the home crowd by taking to the field wearing their home colours of blue and white quartered shirts that clashed with the pale blue colours worn by the Everton players. The Everton players were somewhat confused by the similarity of the Blackburn colours to their own and began the second half wearing black and white stripped jerseys. The skill shown by McDermott, during the game, thrilled the home spectators who cheered Everton on to a 3-1 victory. The Scot held his place in the team until November when he was dropped following a sudden dip in form but returned to take part in the Liverpool Senior Cup final where the opponents were Liverpool.

The match was arranged to coincide with the New Year holiday and both sides placed their strongest eleven in the field. Lord Stanley attended the game along with the large party of guests that he was entertaining at Knowsley Hall. The weather was bitterly cold which kept the number of spectators down to around 20,000. Tom McDermott played his part in an exciting game that was won by Everton by the odd goal in five. Lord Stanley then awarded the trophy to the Everton skipper.

Tommy McDermott, during his first season with Everton, missed just five games as his side finished third in the table. He resigned from Everton next season and was part of the side that was unfortunate not to win the championship. He also took part in an excellent FA Cup run that ended with a defeat by Aston Villa in the semi-final at Trent Bridge Nottingham. All looked well for McDermott when he joined Everton for a third season but, having played just six games, he suddenly left and signed for Division Two side, Chelsea. He had played 71 league and cup games for Everton and scored 19 goals.

McDermott played 32 games and scored 12 goals to help the London club win promotion to the top tier of English football. He left Chelsea after one season and returned to Scotland where he played for both Kilmarnock and Dundee United. Tommy McDermott then ended his playing days back in England with Bradford City.

John Maconnachie ranks highly among the list of players who joined Everton from north of the Border. He was to prove a reliable defender, a redoubtable opponent and an excellent captain. He was born, 8 5 1885, in Aberdeen and is first recorded to be playing football for Glasgow Perthshire, a junior side from the Possill Park area of Glasgow. People from the aforenamed Scottish county who had moved to find work on the Clyde had founded the club. The soccer scouts from Hibernian quickly noticed his commanding displays in the centre half position and he was invited to join the Easter Road club in 1903. Maconnachie made 94 appearances for the Edinburgh side and left them to join Everton following a Scottish Cup semi-final defeat at the hands of Celtic in 1907. He had scored 9 goals for Hibernian, 5 of which had come from the penalty spot.

There were 12,000 people present when Maconnachie made his Everton debut in the reserve derby game against Liverpool at Goodison Park. He was held out of the first eleven by Jack Taylor and Harry Makepeace and had to wait until December to get his chance with the senior side. Maconnachie made his debut, 7 12 1907, and missed a penalty against Newcastle United at St James Park. Nevertheless he played another 20 league games during his debut season yet took no part in a prolonged FA Cup that ended with defeat at Southampton. Maconnachie, in the season that followed, was an ever-present in an Everton that finished runners up to league champions, Newcastle United. He proved to be a versatile defender who was equally at home at full back or in the half back line. John Maconnachie captained the Everton side that narrowly missed out on the league championship in 1912 but at last got his reward when he played a big part in helping Everton to win the league championship in 1914. When World War One broke

74

out he returned to Scotland to enlist but not before playing one match, 15 4 1914, for his old club Hibernian in the Scottish League match against Dumbarton. John Maconnachie, who served with the Royal Flying Corp, survived the conflict and, when hostilities were at an end, headed back to Liverpool where he again signed for Everton. He was appointed club captain in a season that saw Everton flirt with relegation. John Maconnachie played his final game for Everton, 24 4 1920, against Burnley at Turf Moor before being granted a free transfer at the end of the season. The Scotsman scored 9 goals for Everton and had played 275 games in his career that had spanned over thirteen years.

Maconnachie ended his football career with Swindon Town assisting them to become founder members of the Football League Division Three and went on to play 56 league games for the Wiltshire club. In 1922 he moved to Sweden and became manager of the Djugardens IF club in Stockholm and returned to England to manage Barrow in 1927. John Maconnachie died in 1956 at Swindon.

Joseph Donnachie was born in the north Ayrshire town of Kilwinning and first played football with junior side, Rutherglen Glencarin. He later had a short spell with both Morton and Albion Rovers before signing for Newcastle United. He played just two games for the Tyneside club before joining Everton on Friday 16th February 1906.

Joe Donnachie, who could play on either wing, was first introduced to his Everton teammates on the platform at Nottingham Railway Station. The club secretary Mr. Cuff accompanied him and informed them that Donnachie would be playing that afternoon against Notts County at Trent Bridge. Everton drew the game 0-0. Donnachie joined Everton when places on either wing were at a premium and he was constantly overlooked in favour of Jack Sharp and Harold Hardman. He managed to make sixteen league appearances, in two seasons, before leaving Everton to join Oldham Athletic.

The Scot spent the largest part of his football career with the Boundary Park Club helping them to gain promotion to Division One for the first time in their history. He was also, during his time there, selected to play for Scotland on three occasions. He played over two hundred games for the Lancashire club before the declaration of World War I interrupted his career. When hostilities came to an end Joe Donnachie was to be found in Scotland where, 8 3 1919, he first played for Rangers against Hamilton Academicals. He played another six league and cup games for the Ibrox club before spending his second spell with Everton. He went straight in to the first eleven as Everton celebrated the end of war with a home match with Chelsea. He made 16 appearances for the first eleven as Everton, after fighting relegation, ended the season in 16th place. Joe Donnachie then moved to play for Blackpool before ending his football career as player/manager with Chester.

Peter Paterson first played football for the unsually named Royal Albert club in his hometown of Larkhall in south Lanarkshire. Formed by local miners in 1878 the club had originally been of senior status until, in 1927, they went into liquidation to be reformed as junior club. The mines around Larkhall were once owner by a certain Captain Johns, who named the local football club Royal Albert because he owned a boat of that name.

Paterson began playing in an Everton reserve side that was at that time competing in the Lancashire Combination. He made his debut against Rossendale playing at inside forward alongside Sandy Young. Paterson made his first team debut, 5 10 1901, and helped Everton to notch up two points at the expense of Sheffield United. The selectors favoured him for the next four games before he lost his place following a 1-0 win over Stoke. The Everton side, despite their victory, came in for some criticism from the local sports journalists one of whom had this to say...*Paterson like his confederates, made some sad blunders, and altogether the Everton front line shaped about as badly as could possibly be conceived.*

(Liverpool Mercury.) Peter Paterson returned to the reserve side where he remained until the end of season. He then left Everton and joined Grimsby Town.

Adam Bowman was the son of a factory worker who was employed in the local linen industry in the town of Forfar. He was born, 4-8-1880, at 96 North Street and first learnt to play football with St Johnstone before moving across the country to join the East Stirling club in Falkirk. A natural goal scorer, Adam Bowman soon caught the eye of the Everton scouts who captured his signature early in 1901.

He first donned the Everton colours in a friendly game, played at Goodison Park, against the then FA Cup holders Tottenham Hotspur and played a couple of games with the reserve side before making his way into the history books. Adam Bowman made his Everton debut, 25 1 1902, in an FA Cup tie against local rivals Liverpool at Anfield. He is the only Everton player to hold this distinction. He failed to score in the game but Everton, it's safe to assume, would have been happy to come away with a 2-2 draw. Everton, with Bowman in the side, lost the replay by 2 goals to 0. He then took his place back in the reserves. Bowman then had to wait until March 22nd before he made his league debut against Small Heath in Birmingham. He then made another three league appearances, scoring one goal, as Everton were edged out of the title by Sunderland.

Adam Bowman found it difficult to brake in to an Everton forward line that contained such first rate players as Jack Sharpe, Jack Taylor and Sandy Young. He had been selected to play in the first eleven just five times when he decided to leave Everton and join Blackburn Rovers in March 1903. the fee, it was reported, was upwards of £200. Bowman was soon back at Goodison Park scoring twice as relegation threatened Blackburn; they beat Everton by 3 goals to nothing on Easter Monday. A local newspaper had this to say about the game…*On the play the better side won, but Everton displayed form far removed from that which they displayed against Liverpool on Good Friday. At the same time, on one or two occasions during the season they have been really inept so far as the attack was concerned. (Liverpool Mercury 14 4 1903.)* Bowman then score twice as Blackburn won their final game to avoid relegation at the expense of Grimsby Town. Everton, when the season ended, had finished twelfth in table. Rumours then began to circulate in the press that Everton and Blackburn Rovers had squared their game and that Grimsby Town, who were at the centre of the controversy, had been relegated unfairly. The games governing body, decided to take action. The official inquiry, which was held in Manchester, found no evidence of collusion between the players of both Blackburn Rovers and Everton and the league table, it was decided, would remain unaltered. However, Joseph Walmesly, the secretary of Blackburn Rovers, was suspended from any further involvement with football.

Adam Bowman, meanwhile, was to prove a good signing for the Ewood Park club scoring 43 goals in 104 league and cup games he played during the five seasons he spent with them. In 1907 he left Blackburn to join Southern League side Brentford where he remained for one season. He scored 24 goals in 30 games before being persuaded to join Leeds City. He failed to establish a place at the Yorkshire club and returned to Scotland where he played for Leith Athletic before going on to captain his hometown team, Forfar Athletic. Adam Bowman then ended his football career with Accrington Stanley.

Charles Clark was born in the Lanarkshire mining town of Uddingston and joined Everton from Hamilton Academicals where he had been a regular in the half back line. He agreed terms with Everton and signed for them in September 1901.Charlie Clark had to wait until Christmas Day to get his chance of first team football playing at right half in the home game against Aston Villa. He spent two seasons with Everton and was released by the club after making another five appearances in the Football League. Frank Brettell then approached Charlie Clark. It was he who persuaded the Scot to try his luck with the Southern League club. It proved to be a smart piece of business. Charlie Clark served the West Country club from 1903 until 1909 playing, in the process 272 games. Clark then ended his playing career with Crystal Palace in south London.

MERCER'S WORLD-FAMED "PREMIER" FOOTBALL GOODS!!

Opinion of the Everton F. C. on Mercer's Boots.

"The Boots arrived safe. The Members declare that they are really 'Grand,' and in a short time you are sure to get more Orders.—Yours truly, F. BRETTELL, Hon. Sec. Everton F. C."

William McLaughlin was born, 22 6 1882, in Cambuslang and joined Everton, 8 9 1904, having previously played for Hamilton Academicals. He took part in a couple of reserve team games before making his league debut, 10 12 1904, against Stoke at Goodison Park. A local reporter, who watched the game, had this to say about his performance…*evidently he possesses an intelligent appreciation of the niceties of the game, and with more experience of the methods of his colleagues should prove an exceedingly dangerous forward (Liverpool Courier).* McLaughlin next represented Everton in a 2-1 win away at Small Heath before taking part in a rather unusual game against Manchester City, at Goodison Park. Thick fog had, that day, engulfed Liverpool and the selected goalkeeper, Leigh Roose, had not arrived at Goodison Park when the kick off time arrived. Everton nevertheless, took to the field with ten players. Jack Crelly went between the posts until Billy Scott, having changed quickly, replaced him some ten minutes after the kick off. The game ended in a 0-0 draw.

McLaughlin then took over the senior centre forward spot scoring twice in wins over Derby and Notts County before losing his place after a disappointing defeat by Liverpool in the final of the local knockout.

He remained in the reserve side until the final day of the season when he was selected for the first eleven and scored against Nottingham Forest. Retained by Everton, the Scotsman then had to wait until December for his next chance at first team football but was immediately dropped having scored in a 5-2 victory away at Wolverhampton. He failed to win a regular place in a very competitive Everton forward line and was not retained at the end of the season. He had played 15 league games for Everton and scored 5 goals. However, McLaughlin had been popular with the Everton faithful and the local press were there to cover his departure... *Willie McLaughlin and his lady had a very enthusiastic send off on the departure to his home in Scotland from Tithebarn Street station at 12.50 today. Great regret was expressed that the Everton directors had not resigned him and thanks were most heartily tendered to him for the way he had served local football. Enthusiastic in reply, he wished Everton and Liverpool, and to the dear friends he had made in Liverpool. There were cheers from the Everton supporters as the train left the station. (Liverpool Echo, 10 4 1906.)*

McLaughlin had no sooner arrived home than he accepted an offer, made by Frank Brettell, to join former teammate Charlie Clark at Plymouth Argyle. He enjoyed one season with the Devonian club before moving back North to join Preston North End. McLaughlin returned to Scotland in 1911 where he played for his former club Hamilton Academicals before ending his football career with the Shellbourne club in Dublin.

Everton v Liverpool, Villa Park, Birmingham. 31 3 1906

Donald Sloan was a Scottish goalkeeper who arrived at Goodison Park via the Irish League club, Belfast Distillery. He was born 31 7 1883 the son of coal mine fireman in the Ayrshire mining village of Rankinston but no reports of his early football activity have yet come to light. He made his debut against Earlestown at Goodison Park on the day when the Everton first eleven won the FA Cup at the expense of Newcastle United. There was a far bigger than usual crowd who attended the game and all concerned were anxious for news from the Crystal Palace. Next season Sloan settled in to the reserve side and was first called to first team duty in the build up to the 1908 FA Cup final. The Everton directorate had decided to rest five players, one of whom was their goalkeeper Billy Scott, and Sloan deputized for him in the league match against Blackburn Rovers at Ewood Park. He made his home debut two days later against Woolwich Arsenal. The fixture had been scheduled for the April 20th but Everton on that day would be playing, against Sheffield Wednesday in the FA Cup final. Everton beat Woolwich Arsenal 2-1 and Sloan then returned to reserve team football. He spent one more season with Everton and acted on behalf of Billy Scott on four occasions before leaving Everton to join Liverpool at the end of the season. He spent one season at Anfield before rejoining Belfast Distillery as their player/manager. In 1906 Donald Sloan married Edith Page in Belfast and the couple had two children. In 1911 Donald, along with his wife and two children, are counted on the census while visiting the Robertson family who live at 617 High Street Shettleston in Glasgow. He gives his occupation as a coal mine brusher. When the war broke out Donald Sloan enlisted in the army and landed in France 2 10 1915 as private S/9311 serving with the Royal Highlanders. He was killed in action 1 1 1917 and was buried in the Faubourg D'Amiens Cemetery in Arras. The name of this former Everton goalkeeper is recorded on the war memorial, high on an Ayrshire hillside, at the centre of the former mining community where he was born.

Robert Graham was a Scot who arrived at Everton to have his second spell of playing football in England. He was born in 1879 in Glasgow where he played junior football with Cartha before joining the Queens Park second eleven who played under the name of "The Strollers. Graham then spent one season with Third Lanark before heading off to London where he spent one season playing football with Fulham. He then returned to play with Third Lanark from where, during the recess of 1907, he joined Everton and took up the inside forward position with the reserve side.

Rob Graham, during his time at Goodison, was selected to play just one game for the Everton first eleven. It came in a second round FA Cup tie away against Oldham Athletic. The tie, watched by a crowd of 26,000, was a bruising encounter that saw Everton happy to come away with a draw. Rob Graham then returned to the reserve side where he remained until the end of the season. The club did not retain him.

The former Third Lanark man joined Bolton Wanderers from where he returned to his native Glasgow and played football for Partick Thistle. Rob Graham ended his playing days at Perth where he represented St Johnstone.

Alexander Birnie was a right-winger who was born at Aberdeen in 1884. He had previously played a couple of games with Southern League side West Ham United before joining Everton in the summer of 1905. He had to wait until the Christmas holiday before being selected for the first eleven which came in a home game with Bury on Boxing Day. Birnie then took part in another two league games, against Bolton Wanderers and Manchester City, but was not retained by the club at the end of the season. He later joined Norwich City.

Thomas Dilly, the son of a local mariner was born, 1891, at 15 Kyd Street in the Forfarshire fishing port of Arbroath and caught the eye of the Everton directors while the club was touring in Scotland in April 1902. He returned with the Everton party to Liverpool and first played for the club against Glasgow Rangers in a Glasgow Exhibition Cup match that was played, 1 5 1902, at Goodison Park. Dilly, who played on the wing, had already represented Scotland at junior level and was reported to be a promising youngster. He returned to Liverpool next season where he quickly settled in to the second team set up at Goodison Park. The first season Dilly spent at Everton was to be his most successful for he featured in the first eleven on six occasions. He then spent another five seasons with Everton playing the occasional first team game before being released by the club in April 1907.

Tommy Dilly later signed for West Bromwich Albion and spent several seasons with the Staffordshire club. In 1911 he married a lady from Reddith and lived in the Shropshire town of Atcham. Dilly spent the rest of his days in the Midlands and died, aged 73, in Birmingham.

William Black was yet another product of the Lanarkshire coalfield having been born 16 4 1878, at Framlington. He began his career as an amateur with Queens Park before moving across Glasgow to join Celtic in August 1904. Black played 10 Scottish League games for the Parkhead club before moving south to join Everton in May 1905.

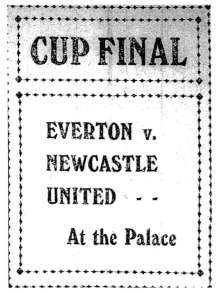

CUP FINAL

EVERTON v.

NEWCASTLE

UNITED - -

At the Palace

He took part in the pre-season trial match where a local journalist was optimistic about his future… *Black, late of Celtic, has every indication of turning out a source of strength in the half back line. His play on the left was very praiseworthy (Liverpool Courier.)* He quickly got a taste of how the game was played in England when he stepped in for the injured Harry Makepeace, 16-9-1905, against Newcastle United at Goodison Park. The former Celtic man did reasonably well during his first season with Everton making several first team appearances late in the campaign. The Scot, during this period, proved to be a great asset to the club as they struggled with the fixture congestion caused by them reaching the final of the FA Cup. Willie Black was retained by Everton and began the next season in the second eleven where he waited until November before being called upon to assist the first team in a 2-1 win at the expense of Blackburn Rovers. He then played a couple of intermittent first team games before helping Everton through the fixture pile up that had been brought on by the club's second consecutive appearance in the FA Cup final. His last appearance for the club was a somewhat low-key affair against a Sheffield Wednesday side that had, seven days previously, beaten Everton in the FA Cup final. The club then retained Willie. However, he never again appeared for Everton because an injury, received outside of the game, forced a premature end to his football career. William Black played 20 league matches for Everton.

Alexander Simpson Young was born in September 1880 at Lochside in the small Stirlingshire town of Slamannan. He was the son of local born coal miner Peter Young and his wife Agnes. Sandy began playing football in the Stirlingshire Junior League from where he was invited to join Scottish League club St Mirren at Paisley. He spent one season with the Buddies before returning home to play regional football with Falkirk. In April 1901 Everton made their first visit to the Falkirk ground and played out a 2-2 draw. The Everton directors were impressed with the form shown Sandy Young who, following a trial period, accepted an invitation to join them next season.

He cut his teeth in the reserve side before making his debut, 28 9 1901, against Aston Villa at Birmingham and immediately returned to the reserves. He then made history by scoring a goal in the first ever FA Cup tie to be played between Everton and Liverpool. Sandy played only a moderate part in his first season with Everton that saw the club narrowly edged out of the league championship by Sunderland. His goal tally increased gradually over the next two seasons 1903-04 as Everton finished third in the table and runners up to Newcastle United in the season that followed. The scoring exploits of Sandy Young had not goneamiss with the Scottish selectors and, 1 4 1905, he won his first International cap against England at the Crystal Palace. His finest moment however came one later year when he lined up with his Everton team mates to face Newcastle United in the 1906 FA Cup at the Crystal Palace in London. The game was 70 minutes old when Sandy latched on to a centre from Jack Sharpe to score the only goal of the game to land Everton the trophy for the first time in their history.

THE SCENE WHEN EVERTON SCORED THEIR GOAL.

Next season Sandy, who continued to find the net for Everton, won his second International cap when he represented Scotland against Wales on the Racecourse Ground in Wrexham. He remained the firm favourite with the Everton fans until his departure for London where he joined Tottenham Hotspur in the spring of 1911. Sandy Young had played 314 league and cup games for Everton and was, to date, the club's leading scorer with 125 goals. The news of his departure, which was anticipated, was recorded in a local newspaper....

The *Everton crowd will miss him – him being Sandy Young, who has left the Mersey city, after a stay of eleven years. No more shall we see the Scot hitching up his "breeks" no more shall we see him guarding the solitary lock of hair that adores his brow. Young will be missed. Long ago I pointed out he was an excellent advertisement for the club, though I realised that his style of play bewildered his opponents, and his own side, and at times he exceeded the reasonable limits of dribbling. Sandy has gone to Tottenham (£700), and has borne out the exclusive statement made by this paper many days ago. (Liverpool Echo, 9 6 1911....)*

The Everton fans however, had not seen the last of Sandy Young and thousands of them turned out to welcome him when, on the opening match of the season, he re-appeared at Goodison Park in the colours of Tottenham Hotspur. When the "immortal Sandy" appeared on the field the reporter, working for the *Liverpool Daily Post* remarked that...*his enthusiastic reception on Saturday must have astonished the Spurs, and proved to the old Blue that he still retains a warm place in Liverpool hearts.* Everton, when the match commenced, had built up a 2-goal lead when they lost their John Maconnachie with an injury. The visitors then hit back and equalized in the dying minutes with a goal that was scored by no other than Sandy Young. The game ended 2-2. Nevertheless Sandy Young, who did not settle in London, soon left White Hart Lane and returned north where he spent one season with Manchester City. He later moved back to Merseyside and played non-league football with South Liverpool.

Sandy Young, his playing days at an end, emigrated to Australia where he bought a block of land next to his brother John in the state of Victoria. The two men, it was reported, frequently argued about the debt of money that was owed Sandy by his brother until, one December morning, things came to a dreadful conclusion. Sandy Young shot his brother and then turned the gun on himself.

A passing neighbour heard the shots and ran to help both men before informing the local police. Sandy was taken to the local hospital where he later recovered but his brother, who was not so fortunate, died of gun shot wounds. Sandy Young was then transferred to Bendigo Jail where he was detained and charged with the murder of his brother.

Sometime later a leading Liverpool newspaper received a visit from two Ladies from north of the Border whose concern for their brother they expressed, it would appear, in a mellifluous Scottish accent. They won the compassion of a local journalist who told his readers of the reason why they had made the long journey to Liverpool.... *I had a visit this morning from the sisters of Sandy Young, two charming Scottish Lassies, who were naturally quite heart broken over the trouble. They wished me to say how much they appreciated the kindly sympathy of the Liverpool football public, with which sympathy they were much impressed. They have come to the city from their home in Avonbridge, Stirlingshire, and I was fortunately able to put them in direct touch with the Everton secretary, Mr. Cuff. I understand that the Everton club is prepared to do anything possible to assist Young's defence and they have already opened up depositions with authorities in Melbourne to that end.*

The Misses Young, in the course of my conversation with them, said that the last news they have of Sandy, is at Christmas when they received a letter from him. He then appeared to be going on all right and there was no indication of anything in the nature of approaching trouble. Sandy, they said, was always of a melancholy temperament, and they added – Whatever he did, he must have been driven to it, for he was always good. Their Mother, they added, who is approaching her seventieth year, was terribly upset by the news, which had reached her through the medium of the newspapers, and concerning which, they have, as yet, not learned anything from any other source.

The sisters interview with Mr. Cuff was of a personal nature, though they informed subsequently that the Everton secretary gave them every assurance that anything the Everton club do in the way of assisting Sandy in his defence, by the way of evidence or any other way, would be willingly done. Both the Misses Young were very much affected by the reception extended to them in Liverpool, to which City they are complete strangers. I took the opportunity of seeing them off to Edinburgh by the 12.40 train, and they again were expressive of their appreciation of the kindly courtesy of the Everton secretary. (Evening Express, 29 1 1916.)

On 21 June 1916, Sandy Young appeared in court to answer the charge of murder. The widow of his brother, Agnes Calder Young, was summonsed to give evidence. She told the court that her husband began dairy farming in Tongela in 1911 and Alexander Young came from Scotland, in 1914, and took the adjoining block. There was frequent friction between the brothers over money matters and the working of the blocks. On the morning of December 1st she heard a shot fired and later saw her husband lying wounded. She also told the court that Alexander had lent John £250 to come to Australia and later had sent him £100.

Alexander Young said on the night before the shooting, "I missed one of my guns and I suspected my brother of having taken it. We had a quarrel about money matters that night and on the 1st December I loaded my gun for protection. I went to the cowshed where I asked him about my money. John got up and attacked me with a shovel. I ran away and he followed. I stopped and said Stand or I will shoot. He made a rush and said come on fire. I fired and he fell. I took the shovel and then went to my house and shot myself. I do not remember anything after that".

The jury later returned a verdict of manslaughter and Sandy was given a period of three years in Bendigo Jail. The Judge, when sentencing him, said he had taken into consideration the affidavits made by persons who knew him in Scotland in which it was stated that Young was subject to fits of temporary insanity. However, the Judge also stated that although he was desirable for the prisoner, during his sentence, to regain his health he warned that if the authorities were satisfied that at the end of three years that his health had been restored, then it was possible that his term may be extended. Sandy then spent nearly three years in jail before being transferred, for a period of recuperation, to the McLeod Prison Farm on French Island off the coast of the State of Victoria.

The next sighting we have of Sandy Young is when he boards the

SS Ceramic at Melbourne for his journey home to Britain. The date is September 1920. He is listed as passenger number 81 and gives his age as 39. He eventually arrived in Edinburgh where he took up residence at 43 Abercorn Terrace and worked in a local quarry. It would appear that, in later life, he was cared for by his sister Helen who lived close by and it is her who notified the authorities of his death on 18th September 1959. Sandy Young died, aged 78, at The Holly Lodge, York Road in Edinburgh and was buried at Seafield Cemetery. There is no headstone on his grave.

**The last resting place of Sandy Young at
Seafield Cemetery, Edinburgh.**

George Wilson was born, 1884, in the Fifeshire town of Lochgelly where he first began playing football with the junior side, Lochgelly Rangers. He later played for both Buckhaven United and Cowdenbeath before joining Heart of Midlothian where he scored on his debut, 9 11 1904, against Port Glasgow Athletic at Tynecastle Park. The Edinburgh team had been enduring a rather bleak period but his was soon turned around when Wilson joined the club. He helped them gain second place in the league and scored the single goal that gave Hearts victory over Third Lanark in the 1906 Scottish Cup Final. He won four Scottish caps during his time at Tynecastle before leaving to join Everton during the summer of 1906. He was to remain just one season.

Everton agreed a fee of £750 to bring George Wilson, along with his brother David, to Goodison Park but it was he who would prove to be the more successful of the two. He made his debut, 3 9 1906, in the record 9-1 defeat of Manchester City and missed only four games in the first half of the season. George Wilson took part in the Merseyside derby game that produced a record crowd of 52,000 and was selected to play for Scotland against England at St James Park, Newcastle. He played in 27 league games and took part in 6 of the 7 FA Cup ties it took Everton to reach the final where they would play Sheffield Wednesday at the Crystal Palace. The local press appeared to be certain that George Wilson would take part in the game and would partner Harold Hardman on the Everton right wing but, at the eleventh hour, the formation of the Everton forward line was changed. Hugh Bolton was selected in favour of George Wilson who never played football for Everton again.

There was some controversy concerning his departure from Everton but he eventually settled in with the Distillery club in the north of Ireland. In 1907 Newcastle United paid a record fee of £1,600 to take Wilson to St James Park. He played over two hundred games for the Tyneside club and assisted them to win both the Football League championship and the FA Cup. George Wilson later returned to Scotland where he played for Albion Rovers, East Fife and became player/manager of Raith Rovers before emigrating to Canada.

David Wilson was one year older than his brother George. He had also played for Lochgelly and Buckhaven Athletic and played, as an amateur, with Gainsborough Trinity before re-joining George at Heart of Midlothian. He made his Everton debut, 17 9 1906, playing, alongside his brother against Notts County at Goodison Park. He played his fifth and final game for the club against Derby County before leaving, at the end of the season, to join Portsmouth.

Daniel Rafferty was born, 25 7 1886, the son of a coal miner, at 112 Ferniegair Rows in the Lanarkshire town of Hamilton. He was noticed by the Everton scouts while playing with Blantyre Victoria from where he joined Everton in the summer of 1907. Signed to back up the forward line, Rafferty had to wait until March 1908 for his chance at first team football when he played in place of Jack Sharpe against Blackburn Rovers at Ewood Park. Everton had been knocked out of the FA Cup, three days earlier at Southampton and there were several changes in the Everton line up. Blackburn Rovers, who took full advantage, won the game by 2 goals to 0. Rafferty however, was again included in the first eleven that took on Birmingham City the following Wednesday afternoon at Goodison Park. The match attracted a crowd of around 12,000 who watched Everton win by 4 goals to 1. The Scot played one more league game, against Manchester United, and was retained at the end of the season. Daniel Rafferty spent another two seasons with Everton and represented them, in total, 7 times. He was not retained by the club and returned to Scotland where he signed for Airdrieonians.

Hugh Adamson was born in the small Fifeshire town of Halbeath, 21 4 1885, and played junior football with Lochgelly before joining Everton at the age of twenty-two. He first represented the club, 2 9 1907, in the local reserve Derby game against Liverpool, at Goodison Park. There was that Saturday, no major game in Liverpool and around 20,000, encouraged by the fine weather, poured through the turnstiles to watch Everton win the game by 3 goals to 1. Adamson continued in the reserve side until the 21st December when he was selected to play for the first eleven against Woolwich Arsenal at Goodison Park. He gave, it was reported, a *very creditable performance* while marking Bertie Freeman prior to him leaving the London side for Everton. Adamson found it hard to break in to an established Everton half line that consisted of Makepeace, Taylor and Abbott, but could always be relied upon when the opportunity presented itself. He stepped in to a despondent Everton side, following their FA Cup exit at Southampton, when they took to the field against Blackburn Rovers wearing red shirts and helped to see the club safely through a tough tail end to the season.

The signing of Valentine Harris later diminished the chances of first team football for Adamson who managed to play just 7 league games during the 1908-09 season. Everton, nevertheless, invited him to represent them in an exhibition match that was to be played against Chelsea, in the Dutch town of Haarlem. Hugh Adamson, who played an excellent game, was awarded with a gold medal as Everton beat the Pensioners by 4 goals to 0. Adamson was retained by the club but took part in only two first team matches in the season that followed. He was, however, invited by the club to join them on a tour of South America where Everton, accompanied by Tottenham Hotspur, played a series of exhibition matches that were designed to popularise the game in both Argentina and Uruguay. The party was away for 14 weeks and arrived home on the third week of July. Hugh Adamson was again retained by the club but left, 15 12 1909, and joined Bolton Wanderers. He had made 25 league appearances for Everton.

George A Couper was utility forward that joined Everton, 2 4 1907, to reinforce the forward line in the weeks leading up to the clubs involvement in the 1907 FA Cup final. He had previously played for Heart of Midlothian. Couper scored in reserve game before making his debut, 8 4 1907, one day later against Blackburn Rovers at Ewood Park. He subsequently put in appearances against Woolwich Arsenal and Derby County but did not accompany the Everton party to the Crystal Palace. George Couper, having agreed to terms for next season, left Liverpool and returned to Scotland. The player was then back in time for the new season where he played in the reserve team derby game alongside his fellow Scots: Hugh Adamson, Rob Graham and John Maconnachie. Couper spent much of the season playing reserve team football until on Good Friday he was suddenly recalled to Everton first team to play against Liverpool in the Merseyside derby game at Anfield. The kick-off time was brought forward to allow Everton time to catch the appropriate train to London where they were due to play a fixture against Woolwich Arsenal at Plumstead. Nonetheless, a capacity crowd of over 42,000 people packed the ground to watch the two sides play out a goal-less draw. Couper was not included in the Everton party who later left for London. His last appearance in the Everton colours came, 23 4 1907, in the final of Liverpool Senior Cup against Liverpool at Goodison Park. George Couper, having previously mulled two chances, scored the final goal that settled the game and landed Everton the trophy with a 2-0 victory. He was not retained by the club and returned to Scotland at the end of the season.

John J.B. Borthwick was born, 15 2 1886, at North Junction Street on the Leith waterfront where his father was a dock worker. He first played football with both Wemyss Violet and Loghgelly United before returning to Edinburgh in 1906 where he signed for Hibernian. He made his debut for the Easter Road club, 4 5 1907, against Hamilton Academicals and represented them in 33 league games and cup games before joining Everton who placed him in the care of the Raw family who lived at 112 Goodison Road.

Borthwick, who played at halfback, was just less than 6 feet tall and weighed in at around 12 stone. He made his home debut, 23 4 1908, in a home game against Sheffield Wednesday. It was the final game of the season and Borthwick was given his chance as the Everton directors gave a well-earned rest to their skipper Jack Taylor. Borthwick then settled in to the second eleven and played only one first team game in the season that followed. His form appeared to have improved during the 1909-10 season and Borthwick, who played 19 times, looked set to be the ideal replacement for the injured Jack Taylor. However, following the signing of Robert Young , he decided to leave Liverpool during the summer of 1911 and try his hand at Southern League football with

Millwall. John Borthwick had spent 4 seasons at Goodison Park and represented Everton in 25 league matches. Nevertheless the bond with his adopted home was now permanent.

The Scot, during his time in Liverpool, had married his landlord's daughter Ruth who bore him a son who they named William. The Borthwick branch of the family then moved to their new home at Egmont Street in the New Cross area of London where John settled in to play football with his new employers. Borthwick had played 14 league and cup games with his new club when the country was thrown into turmoil by the outbreak of the First World War. John Borthwick enlisted in the 17th battalion of the Middlesex Regiment (the footballers; battalion) while his wife and son returned to the family home at 112 Goodison Road, Liverpool. The 17th battalion, meanwhile was posted to France. They saw action in the Battle of the Somme where, on the 31 7 1916, John Borthwick received a gunshot wound to the head and was admitted to the field hospital at Rouen to where his injuries were treated. He was later treated at the Royal Hospital in Chelsea before being sent home to recuperate at Belmont Road Hospital in Liverpool. John Borthwick, now re-united with his family, was discharged from the service and given a war badge to wear to prevent women from handing him a white feather in the street. The family later set up home at 117 Walton Road in Liverpool.

Ernest Pinkney was born, 23 11 1887, of English parentage on Aikenhead Road in the shadow of Hampden Park, Glasgow. His father, who worked on the railway, later moved his family back to England where they took up residence at Garibaldi Street in the town of Hartlepool. Pinkney was spotted by the Everton scouting system while playing football for Northern League side West Hartlepool and accepted the opportunity to play for the club in 1909.

He was immediately placed in the care of Mrs. Mary Gill at 27 Diane Street where he lodged with Everton teammates Billy Lacy and John Magner. Pinkney began his Everton career playing in the reserve side before making his first team debut, 28 3 1910, in the home match against Bury. There were several changes in the Everton team that day as the team selectors rested several players in preparation for the forthcoming FA Cup semi-final against Barnsley. Pinkney, who took up outside right position, showed promise and helped his side to a 3-0 victory. He then made another two first team appearances as Everton finished mid-way in the table. Pinkney was back on the right wing at the start of next season but lost his place to local amateur Arthur Berry after just three matches. He then had to wait until the New Year to make his eighth, and final, appearance for Everton where he scored the second goal in a 2-0 away win against Preston North End. In March Pinkney made his last appearance in the Everton reserve team and was not retained by the club at the end of the season.

Next season he joined Lancashire Combination side Barrow where he remained for two years before moving south to play Southern League football with Gillingham. In 1915 Pinkney moved back to Merseyside and appeared as a wartime guest player with Liverpool scoring 4 goals in 24 regional matches. When peace was restored Ernie Pinkney moved "over the water" and played football with Tranmere Rovers until 1921. He later played for Halifax Town before ending his career with Accrington Stanley.

James McCrorie Gourley was a member of a famous family of football players who lived in the small town of Annbank in the east Ayrshire coalfield. His father, who was also named James, was better known by his nickname of "White" Gourley and it was he who won two Scottish caps while playing for Cambuslang Rangers. James Junior began his football career playing for Annbank on their tiny ground at Pebble Park from where he joined Scottish Division Two side, Port Glasgow Athletic. Here he came to the notice of several of the leading clubs in England.

In September 1909, Gourley signed for Everton who lodged him with Mrs. Joanna Brown who lived off Bullens Road, at 47 Diane Street. He first made a prolonged run in the Combination side before making his first team debut, 19 3 1910, where he scored in a home game against Chelsea and took part in three more league games before the end of present campaign. Next season he became a regular member of the forward line sharing the goal scoring duties alongside Sandy Young. The signing of George Beare from Blackpool later challenged Gourley's place in the side but he still managed, during the course of the season, to take part in 30 league and cup matches. He went on to play 58 league and cup games for Everton and score 9 goals before joining Morton in the spring of 1913.

The former Everton man became a great favourite with the Cappielow Park fans as he served them faithfully for the rest of his career. Gourley later earned himself a special place in local folklore when he scored the only goal of the 1922 Scottish Cup final that gave Morton a victory over Glasgow Rangers. It is, to date, the Greenock clubs only major triumph.

Walter White had twice represented Scotland when he arrived at Everton from Bolton Wanderers in December 1908. The Goodison Park club was at the top of the league when he joined them and the board hoped that the acquisition of such a class player would clinch them the league championship. "Wattie" White was born, 1882, in the Ayrshire lace manufacturing town of Hurlford and played for the local junior side, Hurlford Thistle, before moving south to strengthen a Bolton Wanderers' side that had just been relegated from the first division of English football. He quickly became the pivotal player with the Burnden Park club and helped them to reach the FA Cup final in 1904. He also helped them to regain their first division status two seasons later. In 1907 "Wattie" won the first of his two caps for Scotland when they drew 1-1 with England on the home of Newcastle United at St James Park and won his other cap, also against England, at the home of Dundee United at Dens Park. He made 33 appearances for the Trotters and scored 24 goals before leaving to join Everton.

"Wattie" White made his Everton debut, 12 12 1908, in a 2-1 win over Sheffield Wednesday at Goodison Park but missed the all important "top of the table clash" with Newcastle United on New Years day at Goodison Park. The Geordies beat Everton and set in motion what was to be a disastrous second half of the season. Everton won only 5 of their remaining 17 league matches to finish runners up to their rivals from Tyneside. "Wattie" however, had performed to the best of his ability by representing his new club in 19 league and FA Cup matches and scoring 4 goals in the process. He continued to play good football throughout the subsequent season and played a full part in the club's long FA Cup run that ended with a semi-final defeat at the hands of Barnsley. The signing of George "Teddy" Beare from Southampton, along with improving form of James Gourley, would appear to be a major factor in the board decision to let "Wattie" go from Everton. In October 1910 he excepted an offer to join second division side Fulham and he moved, with his wife and 3 month old daughter Rachel to west London. He had made 52 league and cup games for Everton and scored 13 goals. His story however, does not end there.

"Wattie" White, with his skilful play, became a great favourite with the fans at Craven Cottage and he wore the Fulham shirt on 203 occasions before he retired in April 1923. He was then 40 years and 9 months old and remains, to this date, the oldest player ever to represent the west London club. He died in July 1950 and was survived by his daughter Rachel Hunt who kept on supporting Fulham until she was over 100 years old. Her death in January 2011, was acknowledged in the Fulham match day programme. **Robert Clifford** joined Everton, from Bolton Wanderers, in a transaction that also included Walter White with whom he had appeared in the 1904 FA Cup final. He was born, 21 11 1883, at 43 house, in the Quad Sacra parish of Coylton at Rankinston in south Ayrshire. He was the sixth child of a local Iron Miner who worked for the Glengarnock Iron and Steel Company. He began playing football at the nearby mining village of Trabboch from where he later joined Bolton Wanderers.

The 1911 census list Rob Clifford as a married man was living at 59 Langham Street in Walton. He made his Everton debut, along with "Wattie" White, against Sheffield Wednesday and played at the heart of the defence. He figured regularly in the ensuing season and played a full roll in the FA Cup run that ended with a defeat by Barnsley. The signing of Rob Young greatly lessened his chances of first team football and Rob Clifford left Everton to be re-united, once again, with his friend " Wattie" White at Fulham. He had played 45 league and cup games for Everton without scoring a goal.

Robert Young had previously played for Middlesborough when he joined Everton for a fee of £1,200. His signing lifted more than a few eyebrows because no club had previously paid more money for a defensive player let alone one who had not yet played for his country. Bob Young was born, 1886, in the South Lanarkshire village of Swinhill. In 1906, he is living at Boghill Street, Stonehouse where, he marries his next-door neighbour, Agnes Barnes. Young's footballing talents first came to notice while playing with St Mirren from where he accepted an offer to join West Ham United in 1907 and spent two seasons with the Southern League club. He then moved back north and signed for Middlesborough. He stayed one season with the Teeside club before joining Everton in the summer of 1910.

On his arrival in Liverpool, Robert Young took up lodgings with the Pimbley family at 11 Chepstow Street. He made his debut at Goodison Park where a large crowd had assembled to cast an inquisitive eye over their new signing on the occasion of the annual pre-season practice match. One local newsman described the new player to his readers… *Young is a well-built player, and his forceful methods were greatly admired. He is a player after the style of Jack Taylor his tactics being very similar to those of the veteran centre halfback.* The Scot immediately took over the Everton centre half

Scots children dance during the interval in the Everton-Aston Villa Game to raise a Burns cot at Liverpool

position that had been left vacant due to the injury of Jack Taylor and took part in the opening season game against Tottenham Hotspur at Goodison Park. He quickly formed a half back partnership with Valentine Harris and Harry Makepeace and scored his first goal for the club against Bury. Rob Young played the first thirteen games before, due to a chest injury; he was forced to stand down against Nottingham Forest. He was soon back in action and took part in the exciting FA Cup game with Liverpool which saw Everton win their way through to the 5th round where they were surprisingly beaten, 5-0, by second division side Derby County at the Baseball Ground. The first team appearances of Rob Young became intermittent to wards the end of a season that saw Everton finish fourth in the table. However, the 36 goals they had conceded was less than any other side in the league and when the club directors announced the squad of players that were to be retained for next season, the name of Robert Young was on the list. He was in the side that began the next campaign with a home game with Spurs and then took a painful knock in the second game against Newcastle United and missed the next game through injury. His place was taken at the heart of the defence by local youngest Tom Fleetwood who deputised well for him until his return some weeks later. However, for some unexplained reason, Robert Young suddenly left Everton at the end of October and joined Wolverhampton Wanderers. He had played 41 league and cup games and scored 8 goals.

Thomas Gracie chose to play for Everton in preference to several of the other top class English clubs who were also anxious to engage his services. He was born, 12-6-1889, in the Dennistoun district of Glasgow where he began playing junior football with the Shawfield club before beginning his senior career with Airdrieonians, Gracie then played for both Hamilton Academicals and Arthurlie before settling down for a lengthy period with Greenock Morton. His skills soon aroused the interest of several English clubs while Morton did all in their power to keep him at Cappielow Park. In 1911 Tom Gracie was declared a reserve for the Scottish International side that had been selected to oppose England at Goodison Park. He travelled with the squad to Liverpool where, while staying at the North Western Hotel, the Government officials, who were taking the census, caught up with him and David Hay of Celtic. Tom Gracie, aged 21, gives his occupation as a professional footballer while Hay states that he is a coal miner. It must be safe to assume, after speaking with the Everton directors, that Gracie was persuaded to say that his interests would be better served by remaining at Goodison Park. The young Scotsman was agreeable to the terms offered by Everton and signed on the dotted line.

The Scottish press predicted a bright future for Tom Gracie and considered his qualities second only in stature to Reid of Glasgow Rangers. He went straight into the Everton side and made his debut at Blackburn along with Frank Jefferies who had also recently joined the club from Southampton. Gracie was included in the six remaining league games that were required to complete the season but managed to score only one goal. He also took part in a Liverpool Senior Cup final that was watched by the players of Newcastle United who were in Liverpool to take part in the FA Cup final replay that was scheduled to take place at Goodison Park on the following afternoon. The Everton directorate, following the departure of Sandy Young, increased their forward options by signing Andy Burton from Bristol City along with the Reverend J C Jordan a crack amateur who had previously played football for both West Bromwich Albion and Oxford University. Nevertheless it was Tom Gracie who led the Everton forward line in the opening game of the new season against Tottenham Hotspur at Goodison Park but, after failing to make an impact, he soon found himself back in the reserves. His chances of first team football were further diminished when, on 10th November, Everton paid out a record fee for Frank Bradshaw a goal-scoring forward from Northampton Town. Gracie remained patient in the reserves until he was called upon to assist Everton in completing the punishing fixture programme that had been allocated to them over the Christmas period. They began with an away match at Bury, 23rd of December, from where the party immediately took the train to Darlington where they alighted to spend the night. Here it was discovered that two Everton players, Gourley and Davidson, had picked up an injury and would not recover in time for forthcoming game with Middlesborough that was to be played on Christmas Day. A telegraph was quickly dispatched in the direction of Liverpool requesting that two replacement players, Lacey and Tom Gracie, be sent to Darlington without delay. Both players, who arrived with all haste, spent a quite but enjoyable Christmas Eve with the Everton party before proceeding on to Middlesborough where, with Gracie leading the attack, they drew the game 0-0. Gracie was also in the team when the same two sides met, the next day, in the return fixture at Goodison Park and then featured in the subsequent fixture away against Tottenham Hotspur. Everton then announced yet another new signing. The club surprised the football world by paying out £1.600 to secure the signature of Tom "Boy" Browell and eighteen year old scoring sensation from Hull City. Tom Gracie, who saw no future with Everton, accepted an offer to join Liverpool.

He spent two seasons with Liverpool before returning to Scotland at the outbreak of the First World War where he signed for Heart of Midlothian. He was an instant success with the Tynecastle club and became his country's leading goal scorer. However, after pressure from the media, he volunteered for military service. Gracie was, at the time, living at 63 Slareford Road in the Scottish capital and his record shows he enlisted, 15 12 1914, at 1, Castle Street in Edinburgh. He was placed with the 16th battalion of the Royal Scots Regiment and listed his next of kin as being that of his mother, Harriet Bell Gracie who resided at 31 Duke Street in Glasgow. He was quickly promoted to Corporal and began his basic training while, when possible, also turning out to play football for Heart of Midlothian. It was while on army manoeuvres Tom Gracie became ill and was admitted to the Infirmary in Leeds before later being transferred to Stobhill Hospital in Glasgow where he died and was buried at Craigton Cemetery. He had been in the army for a little over one year and was just 26 years old. The following letter was then sent to the army record office.

D.D.M.S Headquarters, Scottish Command, Edinburgh.

Sir. I have the honour to report that 1902, Cpl, Gracie T., 16th Royal Scots, was admitted to hospital on 15 9 1915 suffering from Herpes. His temperature suggested of Enteric Fever and as a result of blood examinations it was detected on 1 10 1915 that he was suffering from Leucecythaemia. He thereafter became seriously ill and died 23 10 1915. The strong presumptions is that the disease which caused his death was contracted of commenced subsequently to 8th December 1915.

John H Caldwell was a Scottish goalkeeper who came to Everton having previously played for Reading in the Southern League.

He was born, 1886, in the small Falkirkshire village of Carronshore where he played junior football with the Dunipace club before joining the Scottish League side, East Stirlingshire. In 1906 Caldwell is reported to be keeping goal for Southern League side Reading. He had then spent one season with Tottenham Hotspur before returning to Reading where he played 88 league games for the Berkshire club before joining Everton in 1912.

Caldwell was signed as a replacement for the long serving Billy Scott who was about to leave Everton and sign for Leeds City. He first appeared for Everton, 4 5 1912 in the Liverpool Senior Cup final at Goodison Park. The FA had given permission for the game to be played in May, providing the receipts were allocated to the fund that had been set up to aid the victims of the *RMS Titanic* which had recently been lost in the Atlantic Ocean. Both sides agreed to this arrangement and placed the strongest available set of players in the field. John Caldwell kept a clean sheet as the game ended in a goal less draw.

Next season the Scot made his league debut in the opening match of the season that resulted in a 2-0 win for Everton away at Tottenham. Caldwell, it was reported, *was not asked to negotiate a shot that could not be considered dangerous.* He kept goal without a break, for Everton until March, behind an Everton defence that always appeared to be vulnerable without the presence of their captain John Maconnachie. Caldwell finally lost his place following an FA Cup defeat by Oldham Athletic where his weak clearance was said to have led to the only goal of the game. Willie Hodge then replaced him and John Caldwell left Everton to join Woolwich Arsenal at the end of the season.

John Caldwell made 3 appearances for the Gunners before returning to Elm Park to make another 13 appearances for Reading. In 1915 he enlisted in the Black Watch and, after serving with the Regiment in France, he returned home to Scotland.

Andrew Dunseir Burton had already acquired a wealth of experience when he arrived at Goodison Park much of which had been at the top level of English football. He had been born, 28-7-1882,  in the coal-mining village of Aucherderran in the Kingdom of Fife where he played football for both Thompson Rovers and Lochgelly before sampling Scottish League with Motherwell in 1904. He spent one season with the Lanarkshire club and then signed for the Football League Division Two club, Bristol City. Burton made a big impact at Ashton Gate helping the club to gain promotion to the top flight of English football where, during their first season, they narrowly missed out on the league championship. He represented the West Country club in the 1909 FA Cup final where they lost by a single goal to Manchester United. In 1911 Bristol City were relegated back to Division Two and Andy Burton accepted an offer to join Everton.

He made his Everton debut, 2 9 1911, and scored, in the opening match of the season in the 2-2 draw with Spurs at Goodison Park. He then missed a couple of games before returning to score in a 2-0 home win over Newcastle United. Nonetheless he found it difficult to secure a regular place in an ever-changing Everton side and left to join Southern League Reading at the end of the season. Andrew Burton had played in 12 league games for Everton and scored 4 goals.

William Davidson was born, 30 11 1888, in Glasgow and began his playing career, as an amateur, with both Queens Park and Airdrieonians before signing professional forms to play football in England with Middlesborough. He played 19 league and cup games for the Division One club before agreeing to join Everton who paid £450 for his services.

Principally a left-winger, Davidson made his debut for Everton, 2 9 1911 against Tottenham Hotspur and played a big part in a season that saw Everton pipped for the title by Blackburn Rovers. He scored his first league goal against Bradford City in October and his one and only FA Cup goal in the 5th round replay against Bury. William Davidson went on to play 45 league and Cup games for Everton and scored 4 goals before returning to Scotland to play football with St Mirren.

William Hodge made a surprise debut for the Everton Combination side in a friendly match, at Orrell Park, against the Dominion club from Bootle. He was yet another product of the Ayrshire coalfield having been born in the small town of Kilwinning where he began playing football with the local club. Hodge, it was reported, had signed amateur forms with Kilwinning but had been playing non-league football in England just prior to him joining Everton. He was signed as cover for Frank Mitchell and made his first team debut 1 11 1913 against Bradford City and made another three first team appearances before leaving the club following the signing of Willie Fern. His destination was not recorded in the local newspapers.

Frank Mitchell was born, 25 5 1890, in the Morayshire City of Elgin from where his family later moved to Glasgow. Mitchell began playing his football with the local Maryhill club where he impressed the officials of Motherwell Football Club. He signed for the Scottish Division One side and took his place in the second eleven. However, anxious to obtain first team football, he accepted an offer to join Everton.

The Everton timbers had been, for many years, under the protection of Billy Scott but he had now left the club and joined Leeds City. The big Irishman had been a great favourite with the Goodison faithful and finding a suitable replacement was never going to be easy. Mitchell went straight in to the Everton first team where his early performances were favourable to the eye of a local journalist. *The most encouraging feature of Everton's display was the clever work of Mitchell. The young Scottish keeper gives promise of being a custodian of more than average ability, and on Saturday he showed great coolness, and sureness in dealing with all manner of difficult situations. (Liverpool Courier 8-9-1913.)* However, after a poor spell in November, he lost his place to rival Willie Hodge. In December Everton signed Willie Fern from Lincoln City and Mitchell was confined to second eleven. He proved to be a reliable player when, following an injury to Fern, he saved a penalty at the home of Sheffield Wednesday and stood firm as Everton shunted their way clear of the relegation zone. Next season he found himself suddenly thrust into the first team when, following a disastrous home defeat by Oldham Athletic, Everton lost the services of Willie Fern with a dislocated finger. Mitchell then kept goal as Everton gained home wins over both Notts County and Bolton Wanderers before taking part in the FA Cup semi-final defeat by Chelsea at Villa Park.

The outbreak of the First World War then disrupted Mitchell's career and he returned to his native Scotland. When hostilities ended Frank Mitchell returned to Merseyside where he continued to act as replacement for Willie Fern until, at his own request, he was placed on the transfer list. Liverpool quickly came in with an offer that was accepted by the Everton directorate and Frank Mitchell crossed the park to Anfield. He had played 24 league and cup games for Everton. Mitchell remained at Anfield for one season before ending his football career with Tranmere Rovers.

Robert Norris Parker made a terrific impact on the Goodison Park crowd when he signed for Everton in November 1915 following the sudden departure of Thomas Browell to Manchester City. He was born, 27 3 1891 at 27 Denmark Street in the Possilpark area of Glasgow and first came to the public attention while playing football with Glasgow Rangers. In 1911 Robert, now aged 20, is recorded as living in a four-roomed tenement, still in Possil Park, at 218 Saracen Street with his parents and their eight siblings. He lists his occupation as a professional footballer. Parker spent four years with the Ibrox club scoring 19 goals in 20 Scottish League and cup games before signing for Everton for a fee of around £1,500.

Parker scored on his debut against Sheffield Wednesday and hit the first of his seven Everton hat tricks against Manchester United on Boxing Day. He went on to complete 25 league and cup games and the 17 goals, scored by Parker, proved to be vital in preserving the

First Division status of the Everton club. His goal scoring fetes, which occurred in a subsequent season are now part of Everton folklore as he hit 36 goals in 35 league games to help the club win the championship. The British Government then announced an abandonment of all professional sport and Parker returned to Scotland.

The next positive sighting of Robert Parker is when he enlists in the Royal Scots Fusiliers (Labour Corp) on the 11th December 1915 and served with the Regiment until he was discharged, as a private soldier, on the 26th September 1919. The dreadful conflict however, had taken its toll on Parker and robbed him of some of the best years of his life.

His return to Liverpool delighted the Everton fans who flocked to Anfield when, 27 12 1919, he reappeared in the Royal Blue Jersey against Liverpool. The Scot managed to provide them with a goal but it was the home club who won the game. Robert Parker, now 29, never again produced the form he had once shown at Everton and from early November 1920 there was talk of him returning home to play for Partick Thistle. However, he remained at Goodison for a while longer and scored his last two goals, 15 2 1921, against Manchester United before eventually leaving Everton to join Nottingham Forest. Robert Parker had taken part in 92 league and cup games for Everton and scored 71 goals.

He later became the trainer of the Irish League side Bohemians and, after taking up residence in Dublin, was reported to be lying ill and crippled with the pain in his back. It is now believed that Everton directors, having journeyed to Dublin, tended to his needs before returning him to his native Glasgow. Robert Parker died, 28 12 1950, at his home at 94 Morningside Street in the Provan district and was survived by his wife Jeanie. The cause of death was Coronary Thrombosis, Disseminated Sclerosis.

James Gourley scores the first goal for Everton in a 2-1 home win over Bury.

James Hill Galt had had a long and successful football career with Glasgow Rangers when he decided to sign for Everton just prior to the outbreak of World War One. He was born, 11 8 1885 at 15 Vernon Street in the Ayrshire coastal town of Saltcoats where his father earned a living as an engine fitter. The family later moved to the Partick area of Glasgow where James Galt began playing football with Rangers. He made his Scottish League debut in 1906 and quickly established himself at the heart of the Ibrox defence. In March 1908 he won two International caps when represented Scotland against Ireland and Wales respectively. James Galt had played over 200 games for Rangers and helped them to win the league title on three occasions before he decided on a move to England.

The fee was not disclosed when James Galt signed for Everton on the evening of Saturday 9TH May in Glasgow. He was immediately appointed club captain. The Everton directors were anxious to sign a quality replacement for Valentine Harris who had recently decided to move back to his native Ireland and Galt fitted the bill perfectly. He quickly picked up the pace of the game in England and played in every league and cup game until the end of January when he missed the FA Cup tie with Bristol City. Galt then returned to play at Bradford in a game that ended in bizarre fashion. A sports journalist, who travelled from Liverpool, recorded the event... *Everton's experience at Park Avenue may best be described as dire and dreadful. Trained athletes are of course, inured to all kinds of weather, but it is too much to expect human beings to play football in a blizzard of Artic rigour and severity. Such were the conditions at Bradford on Saturday, and the fact that the teams braved these elements for thirty-seven minutes is a fine tribute to their stamina. Incidentally, it is also a tribute to the hardihood of the Yorkshire sportsmen for quite 6,000 of them faced the storm to watch the match, which ought never to have been begun. Everton losing the toss, were set the task of confronting a piercing wind, which carried with it flakes of snow that froze as they fell. (Liverpool Daily Post 15 2 1915.)* The visitors soon found themselves a goal behind before they suffered the loss of their goalkeeper Willie Fern who, after trying to prevent a second goal, collapsed with exposure and had to be carried from the field. Thompson, who took over in goal, then conceded a third goal before two more Everton players, Grayner and Galt, suffered a partial collapse leaving the referee with no choice but to abandon the game. The Everton captain however, recovered in time to take part in next Saturday's FA Cup tie against Queens Park Rangers that had been transferred to the spacious home of Chelsea at Stamford Bridge. The game, won by Everton, turned out to be a rather rough affair that saw James Galt, following an altercation with an opponent, ordered from the field. Everton, who reached the semi-final, were finally beaten by Chelsea at Villa Park, Birmingham. James Galt, in the meantime had missed six league games but returned in time to lead his Everton side as they squeezed past Oldham Athletic and finally brought the Football League championship to Goodison Park. James Galt then returned to his native Glasgow.

In the summer of 1915 Robert Galt enlisted in the army at Glasgow and was placed with the Royal Army Service Corp. He was given the service number 100565 and the attestation was sent the Corp headquarters at Grove Park Barracks in London. Galt, at the time of his enlistment, gives his address as 12 McLean Street, Partick, Glasgow and names his brother Robert as his next of kin. On the 26th April 1916, James Galt reappeared in Liverpool when he represented Scotland in a Military International against England at Goodison Park. He survived the conflict and returned to captain Everton after the war but then returned to Scotland after one season, where he played football with Third Lanark. He later married Thomasina Logan and returned to his trade as motor engineer. At the time of his death, 17 10 1935, Thomas Galt and his wife were living at Burnside Road, Whitecrags, Newton Means in the County of Renfrewshire.

William Brown was the last Scotsman to be signed by Everton before serious sport was suspended for the duration of the war. He was an 18-year-old half back who had previously proved him self to be a fine athlete during his brief football career with Cambuslang Rangers. He spent his opening months in the reserve side before making his home debut, 12 12 1915, when he assisted Everton to a thumping 4-1 win over highflying Manchester City. Three weeks later Billy Brown was back in an Everton side that delighted the Goodison faithful with a 3-0 victory over Newcastle United. His next appearance, however, at home to Notts County, was a more somber occasion that was respectfully acknowledged in a local newspaper... *There were quite a few men in khaki this afternoon at Goodison Park but the men who caught the eye most were a party of thirty who occupied a place in the principal stand. They were soldiers who had been wounded in the recent fighting at Neuve Chapelle, and at the invitation of the directors arrangements were made for them to witness the match. Some limped so badly that they had trouble getting upstairs and were helped by nurses and some had their arms in splints, and one had his head in bandages. But* *despite their suffering they seemed in good spirits and took a lively interest in the match. Evening Express 20 3 1915.)* The sight of so many of their wounded supporters would have no doubt touched the hearts of the Everton team as they treated them to a 4-0 victory with Billy Brown, once again, having a fine game at wing half. He then played his final game, a victory over West Bromwich Albion, as Everton ended the season as champions. Professional Football then came to an end and the existing Football League system was dissolved. The Scottish invasion of Goodison Park was, temporary, put on hold.

Appendix

N. McBAIN

Neil McBain was born, as the mist rolled in from sea, at Campbelltown on the Mull of Kintyre in 1897. He began his playing career with Campbell Academicals for who he appeared in the 1916 Renfrewshire Cup against Neilston Victoria. The game ended in a 1-1 draw. Beresford Park, then the home of Ayr United, was the venue chosen for the re-play and over 2,000 fans crossed the Firth of Clyde on a "Special Ferry" to watch the Campbelltown men lose the game by 2 goals to 1. However, McBain had caught the eye of the Ayr United executive who captured his signature, in a local hotel, just weeks before he was conscripted in to the armed services.

Neil McBain joined the Royal Navy but still managed to make his debut, against Clyde, on the ground of Partick Thistle. He also saw service with the Black Watch before returning to play football

THE GOODS AT GOODISON. — Chadwick, Irvine, and M'Bain (Everton) waiting for Chedgzoy's centre in the Notts Forest match. Goodison supporters on Saturday forgot all the bad things they said about the team last season.

for Ayr United in 1918 where he was to play 120 league and Cup games and score eight goals.

His many fine performances for "The Honest Men" prompted Manchester United, in November 1921, to pay £4,600 for his signature but he could not prevent them from being relegated to Division 2 at the end of the season. It was during his time in Cottonopolis that he won the first of his three International caps when he was selected to play for Scotland against England at Villa Park. Neil McBain played 42 games for the Manchester club scoring two goals in the process. He became a firm favourite with the fans at Old Trafford who aired their displeasure when he was transferred to Everton, for a fee of £4,200, in January 1923.

McBain joined Everton two weeks after they had been eliminated from the F.A. Cup by Bradford Park Avenue and the Goodison faithful were not in happy mood. His first game for his new club was a friendly game against Stockport County at Edgeley Park where Everton lost 1-0. McBain made his Goodison debut on the 12th February and played his part in a 3-1 victory at the expense of Chelsea. He quickly formed a partnership with club captain Hunter Hart in an Everton half back line that also included Danny Reid. On the 3rd March McBain was again selected to represent Scotland in their fixture against Northern Ireland at Windsor Park and played in every Everton league match from then until the end of the season. During the 1923/24 season he played 39 league and cup matches for Everton while on 16th February 1924, he won his third and final cap for Scotland against Wales at Ninian Park. Next season Neil McBain took over the role of club captain when a serious injury forced Hunter Hart on to the sidelines. Indeed, it was he who captained the side when, in March 1925, a certain W.R.Dean made his debut for Everton against Arsenal at Highbury. Hunter Hart was back leading the team when they returned to Highbury next season and saw McBain score his one and only goal for Everton. He had made 103 league and cup appearances for the Goodison Park club before moving, in the summer of 1927, to join St Johnstone.

In March 1928, now aged 32, McBain made a surprise return to Merseyside and signed for Liverpool where he played 10 leagues matches, at right back, and helped them to avoid relegation. He then joined Watford as player manager and later took charge at Luton Town before returning to live in Ayr where he worked as a joiner for the duration of the Second World War.

In 1946 he again returned to Merseyside this time to become the manager of third division New Brighton. On the 15th March 1947 three of the New Brighton players, one of whom was the goalkeeper, got stranded en route to a match at Hartlepool and Neil McBain was forced to think on his feet. He quickly signed up two young members of the Harlepool United playing staff and named himself to the match officials as the New Brighton goalkeeper. Neil McBain, who completed the match, found his way in to the history books. He was, at the time, 51 years 4 months old and remains the oldest player ever to have taken part in a Football League match. In 1951 he became manager of Leyton Orient before moving on to take charge at Estudiantes in Argentina. In 1955 McBain returned home to manage Ayr United and took them to promotion at his first attempt. He later had a second spell at Watford before returning again to manage "The Honest Men" where he retired, from football, at the age of 68. In May 1974 Neil McBain died at his daughter's home in Ayr. He was 78.

England v Scotland

In 1893 the Football Association decided to play the annual England v Scotland International match at Goodison Park. The new grandstand, built along Bullens Road, had just been completed and the facilities it provided were second to none in England. Jonny Holt was the only Everton player selected to play for England while Edgar Chadwick, who expected to play, had been left out in favour of Cunliffe Gosling. The Scottish F.A. had not yet recognized professional football and their side consisted only of home based amateur players. The teams were selected up as follows:

England: Sutcliffe, (Bolton Wanderers) Lodge, (Cambridge University), Reynolds (W.B.A.) Holt (Everton), Needham (Sheffield United), Bassett (W.B.A.) Bloomer (Derby County) Goodall (Derby County), Gosling (Old Etonians), Smith (Aston Villa).

Scotland: McArthur (Celtic), Drummond (Rangers), Doyle (Celtic), Russell (Hearts), Simpson (3rd Lanark), Gibson (Rangers), Lambie (Queens Park), McPherson (Rangers) Oswald (St Bernard's), Waddell (Rangers), Guilliland (Rangers).

Both sides arrived in Liverpool on Friday evening. The England put up at the Alexandra Hotel in Dale Street while the Scots made their headquarters at the Crompton Hotel in Church Street. The next day they donned their navy blue jerseys and boarded the horse drawn carriage that had been placed at their disposal. The large crowd then looked on as the visitors paused for a team photograph at a studio in Bold Street before making their way up to Goodison Park where their hosts were there to greet them. The England team, as the Scots, arrived, could be seen posing for a photograph on the Everton training ground.

The Scottish fans, having made an overnight journey, began arriving at Liverpool Exchange Railway Station on the seven special excursion trains that been provided for them by the Caledonian Railway Company. The English Railway companies had also capitalised on the occasion and special excursion trains arrived in Liverpool from as far away as London. The crowds made their way up to Goodison Park early hoping the see the local cup final, between Fir Grove and Hawthorne, which had been arranged to precede the main event. However, the morning had been showery, so much in fact that an Emergency Committee, having walked the ground, decided that the game was not allowed be played. The press box was in those days, located in the pavilion located at the top of the high bank of cinders that ran along the Goodison Road side of the ground. The Liverpool newspapers were well represented along with our friend from the Glasgow Herald who, when two Highland Pipers appeared from the crowd, quickly put pen to paper…

Their progress around the field was a signal for unbounded enthusiasm; indeed it savoured a Royal entry in to this city. It must be admitted that their presence created the necessary enthusiasm to a great occasion and both English and Scotch were for once hard as fast friends. As the hour wore on, the space in front of the press box presented a sight similar to that seen on a great race day. Men in fustian and corduroy mixed with theatrical managers and merchants who paid their nimble sixpence, preferring to take advantage of the high ground to having a seat on the reserved benches. Splendid arrangements were made by the Post Office to cope with the enormous number of messages, which were to be sent to the Telegraph Office in cabs every fifteen minutes At two minutes past four Gosling led on his men and was received with great shout, the ever popular Holt being marked out as the one local man. This was very flattering to the English; but their reception was nothing to that which greeted the champions of the Thistle, who came out a few minutes later. The Scotsmen fairly rose to the occasion, waving handkerchiefs, hats and "bonnets" and cheering lustily. It was twelve minutes past the hour when Oswald and Gosling tossed for the choice of positions, the former, with the wind in his favour, taking the town goal. It was observed that Danny Doyle was a last moment substitute and this change gave general satisfaction quite as much to the Dicky Sams (The word Scouser, not yet in fashion) *who had very pleasant recollections of that sterling player - as do the Glaswegians who were present.*

The roars from the Scots, it would seem, had little effect on an English team that was led by their aristocratic captain Cunliffe Gosling and it was a foul, committed against him, that led to the opening goal. The free kick, well taken by Jonny Holt, landed at the feet of Steve Bloomer who scored for England after 25 minutes. The goal seemed to invigorate the home forwards who again put great pressure on the Scottish defenders. This caused them to panic and Gibson, in his over anxiety to clear, sliced his kick past his own goalkeeper for a second goal to England. The Scots' troubles were then trebled when, two minutes before the break, a misplaced clearance from Drummond went straight to Smith who scored to give England a 3-0 lead at the interval.

Still our friend from the Glasgow Herald, who stuck cheerfully to his task, continued to record the events for his readers…The *usual interval was taken advantage by the so called "Glasgow Choir" in the reserved seats to give the public the benefit of a lusty rendition of "Scots whae hae" to which the Englishmen responded by saying that they would bleed Wallace and his men to another tune before the day was out.*

Rain had started to fall as play recommenced but both sets of supporters remained in good spirits. The game, as play wore on, slowly drifted away from the Scots and a local reporter recorded the closing stages of the game. *At this particular period it appeared that it was only a question as to how many goals the Englishmen would win by. The Sun now broke forth and rendered matters more comfortable for the onlookers (Liverpool Courier.)* The home side finished much the stronger of the two teams and only some stubborn defending by the Scots prevented them from adding to their score as the game finished, England 3, Scotland 0. There was a crowd of 42,000 people who watched the game and they generated record receipts at the gate. This was to date, the largest crowd to watch an International match in England. Nevertheless, it would be another 16 years before the game was again played in Liverpool.

There had been several improvements made to Goodison Park since the Scots had last visited the location and the first of these was an elevated grandstand, seating 2,600 people, that had been sited, in 1906, at the Stanley Park end of the ground. The most dramatic changes however, had taken place along Goodison Road. Here a gigantic new grandstand, the highest in the country, had been constructed to bring the capacity of the ground up to an estimated 70,000. The Scottish F.A. had now changed its attitude towards professional football and was prepared to select players who were earning a living outside of their homeland.

It was around lunchtime when the Scottish party left Glasgow on a train that stopped at Carlisle to pick up their three Newcastle  based players. They arrived at Exchange Station in Liverpool and immediately took the electric train to Southport where they spent the night, along with their opponents, at the Queens Hotel. The visiting fans soon began arriving in Liverpool on the 15 special trains that had left Scotland. They were in high sprits as they began to collect outside the Everton ground and this picture (Left) records the occasion. Flat caps are very much in evidence as these football fans of yesteryear cheerfully pose for the camera. Lord Derby, along with the Lord Mayor of Liverpool, looked down from the high balcony as the teams took to the field from beneath them. Over 50,000 spectators where in the ground and the gate receipts established a new record for a football match in England. The teams lined up as follows.

England: Williamson (Middlesborough), Crompton (Blackburn Rovers), Pennington (West Bromwich Albion), Warren (Chelsea), Wedlock (Bristol City), Rev Hunt (Leyton), Simpson (Blackpool,) Stuart (Newcastle United), Webb (West Ham United), Bache (Aston Villa), Evans (Sheffield United).

Scotland: Lawrence (Newcastle United), Coleman (Aberdeen), Walker (Swindon Town), Aiken (Leicester Fosse), Low (Newcastle United), Hay (Celtic), Bennett (Rangers), McMenemy (Celtic), Reid (Rangers), Higgins (Newcastle United), Smith (Rangers).

The early exchanges were of an even nature before some shoddy defending, by the Scots, led to the first goal. Both full backs, in turn, missed their chance to clear before Stewart, who scored with a low shot, gave England the lead on 28 minutes. Scotland then had a goal disallowed when a shot, delivered by Higgins, appeared to rebound from the side of the net near to the goal post. It then struck goalkeeper Williamson and rolled out of play. The Scottish players appealed franticly for a goal but the referee, Mr. Nunnery of Wales, would not listen and awarded them a corner that was cleared by England. The crowd was still debating the incident when the half time whistle sounded. The first chance of the second half fell to England but Bache failed to capitalize up on his opportunity. The England captain, Bob Crompton, was having a fine game as his side edged ever closer to victory. The game appeared to be going away from the Scots until, with two minutes remaining, Smith picked up the ball on the left wing. He beat two men and centered for

Higgins to head his side level. The game ended in a 1-1 draw. The two sides later spent the evening in Liverpool where they observed to be watching a Bioscope show at the Olympic theatre on West Derby Road. The event "which went of without a hitch, had been a great success.

Dixie's Day at Hampden

On 2nd April 1927 Everton Football Club were forced to play out a 0-0 draw away match at the Derby without the services of their new goal scoring sensation who was away on International duty. Dixie Dean was just 20 years and 2 months old when he was picked to lead England against Scotland at Hampden Park in Glasgow. There were reported many Lancastrians amongst the large number of English fans who arrived at Glasgow Central Railway Station where the staff were on hand to redirect them on the numerous local railway trains that would ferry them out to Mount Flordia. The fans poured out of the station and crossed the busy Cathcart Road where a continuous fleet of tramcars, nearly 300 in number, was also busily engaged in transporting the fans to the famous stadium from all parts of Glasgow. They poured through the turnstiles and filled the vast amphitheatre that had been opened in October 1903. The Scots were thought to be a much more experienced side and England was given very little chance of victory. The roar that greeted the teams must have rung in the ears of the young Dixie Dean he lined up with the English players and set the game in motion. The teams had lined up as follows:

Scotland: J. Harkness (Queens Park), W. McStay (Celtic) R. Thompson (Falkirk), T. Morrison (St Mirren), J. Gibson (Partick Thistle), J. Mullan (Manchester City), A, McLean (Celtic), A. Cunningham (Rangers), H. Gallagher, (Newcastle United), R. McPhail (Airdrieonians) and A. Morton (Rangers.)

England: J. Brown (Sheffield Wednesday), F. Goodall (Huddersfield

Town), H. Jones (Blackburn Rovers), W. Edwards (Leeds United), J. Hill (Burnley), S. Bishop (Leicester City), J Hulme (Arsenal), G. Brown (Huddersfield Town), W. Dean (Everton), A. Rigby (Blackburn Rovers) and L. Page (Burnley).

"Dixie" Dean, of Everton, harassing the Scottish goalkeeper in the International match at Glasgow. He played a brilliant game and gave England the victory by scoring both goals.

Things quickly began to go wrong for the visitors when their captain Jack Hill collided with a teammate and had to be carried from the field with a gash to his forehead. He then had three stitches inserted in his wound and was warmly applauded when, with head swathed in bandages, he returned to the field took and up position on the wing. The English quickly re-organized their defence as the Scots piled on the pressure but no goals had been scored when the half time whistle was heard. Hill re-appeared for the second half but had to leave the field again to have his head re-dressed and it was during his absence, that the Scots took the lead thanks to a headed goal from Alan Morton. The England captain then returned to field where he continued to rally his men from his position on the wing. His words of encouragement must have reached the ears of the young England centre forward who, on 75 minutes, latched on to a long ball that had been cleared from out of the defence. He powered his way between the Scottish full backs to beat goalkeeper Harkness with a low drive into the corner of the net. Minutes later England appeared to have taken the lead when a centre from Page appeared to sail through the hands of Harkness and into the net. The vast crowd, who now numbered 111,145, sighed with relief when Dean was adjudged to have fouled Harkness and the goal was disallowed by the referee. Their relief then turned to disbelief when, with two minutes left to play Dean took advantage a of mix up in the home defence to prod ball the past Harkness and into the net. Two minutes later the sound of the final whistle signalled a famous victory for England. Dixie Dean was the hero of the hour but the fortitude shown by Jack Hill had proved a great inspiration to his England teammates.

It had been great day for the young Dixie Dean who, next season, would score a record breaking 60 goals for Everton as they went on to win the championship. He would however, never score against Scotland again. England would now have to wait until the 15th April 1939 before they would taste victory at Hampden Park again when trailing to an early goal; they again hit back to win by 2 goals to 1. A 19-year-old centre forward from Everton supplied the winning goal that was scored two minutes from the end. His name was Tommy Lawton.

Wartime International

On the evening of Saturday 13th May 1916 a specially arranged International soccer match took place at Goodison Park between two teams of servicemen who represented England and Scotland. The game kicked off at 6 p.m. and the participating players had been granted leave by the military authorities. The local papers omitted to give the result but stated that the game yielded full satisfaction from the playing point of view and that the football was of a skilful nature.

England XI: Private A. Robinson (Blackburn Rovers), Gunner L. C. Weller (Everton), Private I.Boocock (Bradford City), Corporal L. Adams (Chelsea), Gunner T. W. Boyle (Burnley), Private J. Brennan (Manchester City), Airman F. Walkden (Tottenham Hotspur), Corporal C. Buchan (Sunderland), Private H. Hampton

(Aston Villa), Bombardier J. Smith (Bolton Wanderers) and Private E. Mosscrop (Burnley).

Scotland XI: Corporal J. Campbell (Liverpool), Trooper W. Henry (Manchester City), Farrier-Sergeant Frew (Hearts), Lieutenant Logan (Raith Rovers) Sergeant J. H.Galt (Everton), Private J. Scott (Leeds City), Sergeant J. G. Reid (Airdrieonians), Gunner A. Cunningham (West Ham United), Gunner W. Reid (Glasgow Rangers), Private P. Allan (Clyde) and Private W. Wilson (Hearts).

The Lord Mayor of Liverpool later that evening entertained the players and officials to dinner at the Adelphi Hotel. His Worship, speaking after the meal, informed those present that the game had raised £1,000 and this amount was later presented by Everton Football Club to Liverpool Stanley Hospital. The money was used to endow a bed at the hospital and a plaque, in accordance with the club's wishes, was fixed at the bed' head. The hospital treasurer, Mr. Oswald Dobell, acknowledged the kindness shown by the directors of Everton Football Club.

Liverpool Caledonians

The Liverpool Caledonian Football Club was the brainchild of Robert Kirkland, a Scotsman who had chosen to make his home in Liverpool. He was born, 1865, in Airdrie from where he had moved south and set up the Vienna Bakery Company on Hardman Street in Liverpool. Mr. Kirkland was keen on sport and was prepared to aid the local Scottish community in the formation of an association football club. The team, formed in 1891, adopted the name of Liverpool Caledonians and Mr. Kirkland was appointed to the role of club president.

The new club purchased a large house and grounds that stood on the east side of Smithdown Road. The location was called Woodcroft. The Scottish community quickly adapted the site to suit their needs by enclosing a football pitch and erecting a small covered grandstand. They decided to call the ground, Woodcroft Park and immediately began to recruit a set of players from amongst the local community. George Farmer, Daniel Kirkwood and W.H Parry, who were signed from Everton, joined the new club along with Lanarkshire born William Hastings who had previously played for Bootle. The Deighton brothers were the next players to sign for the Caledonians having also previously played at Bootle. The other recruits appear to be Scotsmen who were resident in or around Liverpool.

The enclosure was officially opened on the Monday 28TH September 1891 with a football match against the Everton second eleven. The occasion attracted at crowd of around 3,000 people who watched the visitors win the game with a single goal that was scored by Thompson. The action then shifted to the Bee Hotel in St Johns Lane where the first team players of both Bootle and Everton were amongst the 100 people who sat down to consume an excellent dinner that had been provided by the local Scottish community. Several toasts were then proposed, and duly acknowledged, before the evening ended with musical entertainment.

Liverpool Caledonians now took their place on the second tier of English football and arranged home and away fixtures with the reserve sides of the senior football clubs from both Derby and Nottingham. Games with Bangor, Tranmere Rovers and Wrexham were also arranged and plans put forward to improve the facilities at Woodcroft Park. The Caledonians then welcomed in the New Year with games against two sides that were visiting England from Scotland. Cowlairs, a team from Glasgow, beat them 4-2 while the game against Airdrieonians ended in a 2-2 draw. The return game with Everton reserves took place at Anfield in February where a crowd of 4,000 watched the Caledonians beaten by 5 goals to1. The Liverpool Scots then took part in the Liverpool Challenge Shield. The competition was contested between the sides that had been beaten in the preliminary rounds of the Senior Cup and the Caledonians defeated both Earlestown and Prescot to set up a final clash with Southport Central. The game took place at Woodcroft Park where a crowd of nearly 4,000 people watched Liverpool Caledonians take the trophy with a 2-1 victory. This success encouraged the local Scots to continue with their plans for the future.

The summer of 1892 saw certain executive members of Everton FC decamp from Anfield and move to a new home at Goodison Park while those who remained behind, formed Liverpool Football Club. The new club, along with Liverpool Caledonians applied to join the Football League when their annual meeting took place at the Bell Hotel in Sunderland. Newcastle East End and Middlesborough Ironopolis also had their applications on the table. All four sides had the application rejected. Liverpool Caledonians, along with their neighbours from Anfield, then successfully applied to join the Lancashire League.

The exiled Scots now formed themselves into a limited company that was registered with a capital of £5,000 in £5 shares. This enabled them *to purchase, lease, or otherwise acquire and hold land in or near Liverpool suitable for a football ground or other sports and outdoor games, and to carry on the business of an athletic company in all its branches. The number of directors is not to be less than three or more than seven. They set up offices at 32 St Johns Lane.* The Caledonians added to their programme of Lancashire League fixtures by successfully applying to compete in the F.A. Cup, the Lancashire Cup and the Liverpool Senior Cup respectively. A covered terrace had now been added to Woodcroft Park while the football pitch had been encompassed by a cycle track. Everything appeared to be well in order as the 1892/93 football season commenced.

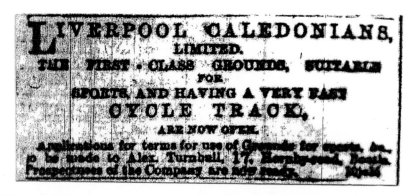

The Caledonians got their Lancashire League campaign off to a good start with a 5-1 win over Rossendale before entertaining Blackpool at Woodcroft Park. The match "pulled in" a crowd of over 2,000. The Seasiders arrived late and annoyed the clientele by taking to the field forty minutes after the time advertised for the kick off. The visitors, having taken an early lead, were then put under constent pressure by the home side. Nevertheless, the Caledonians failed to score and two late goals, scored by the visitors, gave a false impression to the manner in which Blackpool had achieved their victory. The Caledonians were then eliminated from the Lancashire Cup by South Shore at Blackpool before turning their attention to qualifying for the national knockout. They were placed in division seven along with such clubs as Bootle, Chester, Liverpool and Northwich Victoria. The Caledonians enjoyed an easy first round win over Wrexham before facing neighbours Bootle in round two at Hawthorne Road. The crowd, who numbered around 3,000, was surprised to see the visitors win the tie by the odd goal in five. The victory gave the Caledonians a round three home tie with Chester who they also beat by 3 goals to 2. The club, in the meantime, made what was to be their one and only visit to Goodison Park. The occasion drew at crowd of around 2,000 who saw the Everton reserve side win the game by 4 goals to 0. Everton, when the return game took place, took the field with a side that included five of their first team players. The game drew a record crowd of over 4,000 people to Woodcroft Park who watched the Caledonians hold their neighbours to a 1-1 draw. An away victory over South Shore lifted the Caledonians to fourth place in the Lancashire League the week before their next F.A. Cup tie against Northwich Victoria.

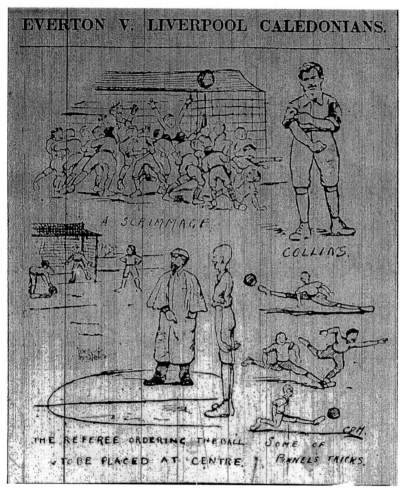

Things appeared to be going reasonably well on the football field but behind the scenes the canny Scots were heading for a financial crisis. Money was in short supply and the club was tottering on the brink of extinction. Their unstable situation quickly reached the ears of the press and the following article appeared in a local newspaper…*Scotchmen are proverbally a hardheaded race, and*

will not be beaten if anything in the way of perseverance and precaution can prevent it. The Liverpool Caledonians were lately threatened with extinction and altogether showed grave symptoms of chronic debility and dissolution, but in the midst of their trouble an enterprising spirit has come forward for the honour and glory of his country. As announced elsewhere the Caledonians meet Northwich Victoria at Woodcroft Park and it is to be hoped that Scotsmen will rally in their thousands to support a combination which at any rate has the courage to adopt a title which approaches consistency in its personnel. (Liverpool Courier.)

LANCASHIRE LEAGUE.
Results of matches played up to Saturday last :

	Played	Won	Lost	Drn	For	Agst	Pts.
Bury	10	8	2	0	37	18	16
Liverpool	8	7	1	0	33	5	14
Blackpool	8	7	1	0	30	12	14
Liverpool Caledonians	7	3	2	2	14	12	8
Heywood Central	7	4	3	0	21	19	8
South Shore	8	2	2	4	25	22	8
Fairfield	9	2	3	4	16	21	8
Fleetwood Rangers	7	3	3	1	17	23	7
Southport Central	9	3	6	0	15	17	6
Rossendale	8	2	5	1	16	21	5
Higher Walton	11	2	8	1	15	51	5
West Manchester	7	1	4	2	15	25	4
Nelson	7	1	5	1	15	24	3

The call, alas, went unheeded and there were only around 1000 spectators present when the teams lined up to face each other at Woodcroft Park. The Salt miners, who had knocked out Liverpool in the previous round, began the game with the stiff breeze in their favour. Hargreaves had given them the lead before a goal from Bryce brought the home side level at the interval. The visitors re-took the lead when Will Parry headed the ball past his own goalkeeper but Bill Hastings, with a last minute equaliser, took the game in to extra time. The hopes of the home club then faded with the daylight when, somewhere in the gloom, Northwich Victoria scored the goal that finally ended any hopes they had of a lucrative F.A Cup run. Liverpool Caledonians had reached the end of the road and a fond farewell was now imminent.

The executive called the players together and informed them of their intention to "wind up" the club and that they must look for somewhere else to play their football. Indeed, so swift was their action that it went unnoticed by Warrington AFC who, one week later, arrived to fulfil a pre-arranged fixture at Woodcroft Park to find the place deserted. Liverpool Caledonians also withdrew from the Lancashire League and their record was expunged while Woodcroft Park was sold and given over to housing. Robert Kirkland continued to run the Vienna Bakery on Hardman Street until, after being taken over by Scots Bakery, it was eventually closed down. The premises then became Kirkland's Wine Bar before changing its name to the "The Fly in the Loaf".

EVERTON FOOTBALL CLUB.
On the GOODISON ROAD GROUND,
MONDAY NEXT, SEPTEMBER 19,
RESERVE v.
LIVERPOOL CALEDONIANS.

The Falkirk Connection

Falkirk Football Club, which was formed around 1876, played on several locations before finaly settling in 1882 at Brockville Park. The club nickname, The Bairns, is determined by a local folk tale that told strangers it was *"Better to meddle with the Devil, than with the Bairns of Falkirk"*. However, Devil or no Devil the Bairns of Falkirk were to develop a strong link with the "Toffeemen" of Liverpool.

It was Monday 29th April 1901 when the players of Everton Football Club first took to the field to oppose a Falkirk side that, at the time, played their football in Central Combination of Scotland. The visitors, who fielded a couple of reserve team players, gave a trial game to two young Scottish junior players. They were Sharp of Burnbank Athletic and Knox of Glenbuck Juniors. The home side, which had the better of the early exchanges, took the lead after twenty minutes when their centre forward Sandy Young *drove the ball hard in to the off corner of the net.* Everton then drew level when, following a save by the home goalkeeper, Knox scored with a simple header. The play then changed direction. The home side had easily the best of their League opponents after the resumption, but had hard lines at goal. Eventually, with fifteen minutes left to play, Falkirk retook the lead with a goal from Webster. The crowd, who numbered 1,500, sensed a home victory but Everton were not yet beaten and rallied strongly and forced a corner in the last minute of the game. The everdependable Jack Taylor headed home the centre, taken from the left, to earn Everton a 2-2 draw. Everton, following the game, offered a trial period to Sandy Young and after obtaining his signature, agreed to return to Brockville Park the following season.

The Bairns of Falkirk joined the Scottish League in 1902 and were promoted to the top flight three years later. Next season the club suffered a set back when a disastrous fire completely destroyed their grandstand. In 1913 the Bairns achieved their first major success when, at the expense of Raith Rovers, they lifted the Scottish Cup at Celtic Park in Glasgow. In 1922 Falkirk astounded everybody by paying a world record fee of £5,000, for the services of Syd Puddefoot from West Ham United who remained at Brockville for three seasons before joining Blackburn Rovers. The Falkirk supporters then had to endure many lean years until their favourites again reached the Scottish Cup in 1957. They drew 1-1 with Kilmarnock, at Hampden Park, before winning the replay, at the same venue, by 2 goals to 1. The club has won nothing since.

The Bairns battled on through many lean years that followed their cup win and their efforts were at last rewarded when, in 2005, they won promotion to the Scottish Premier League. Their Brockville ground however, was below the required standard and their entry was denied. The local council, in conjunction with the club, then decided to build an impressive new ground that was to be called "Falkirk Stadium". The Bairns, who were temporarily homeless, shared the home of Stenhousemuir at Ochilview Park until their new ground was complete. In 2005 Falkirk at last won promotion to the Premier League and a new era began at their impressive new home. The location contains a spectacular new grandstand complete with a top class restaurant; conference centre and function suit. The ground capacity, which stood at 6,800, was then increased by the opening of a new stand behind one the goals.

The Bairns, over the years, have developed strong links with Everton as Alex Parker, "Mo" Johnson, John McLaughlin and David Weir have all arrived at Goodison having previously played their football at Brookville Park. The old Falkirk ground however is assured a place in Scottish folklore when the ball, during a home match, was kicked over the periphery of the enclosure. It fell directly on to the wagon of a goods train that was, at that moment, passing the ground and "disappeared in a puff of smoke". The Falkirk executive, after checking with their local goods depot, discovered that the train was bound for Perth and promptly dispatched a member of their committee off in that direction. The canny Scot arrived at Perth and, after searching the railway sidings, found the ball and brought it back to Falkirk. It was later estimated that it had travelled a distance of 43 miles thus making it the "longest kick" in the history of Scottish football. Sandy Young however, was not thought to be responsible.